*Dear Robert,
bless you richly and
Best regards!*

PEACE UNDER THE ROOF
A Korean Love Story

BY GEORGE J. ADAMS

George Jacob Adams

Fairway Press
Lima, Ohio

Dec. 1992

PEACE UNDER THE ROOF

FIRST EDITION
Copyright © 1992 by
George J. Adams

All rights reserved. No portion of this book may be reproduced or utilized in any form or by any means, electronic or mechanical, including photocopying, without permission in writing from the publisher. Inquiries should be addressed to: Fairway Press, 628 South Main Street, Lima, Ohio 45804.

7922 / ISBN 1-55673-470-0   PRINTED IN U.S.A.

This Book Is
DEDICATED

To my very dear sister, Dorothy Dick Adams, who mothered me from the time I was barely two years old and lost my mother, the Ahn Lady of this story, until my step-mother took over, when I was five. Also, quite recently, if Dorothy hadn't stepped in and helped, the manuscript of this book might still be batting from pillar to post.

Blessings on you, Sister Mine. You are an angel, without much disguise.

Your loving brother-author.

Table Of Contents

I	Kee-haw's Big Decision	11
II	New House	23
III	Weapon: Dining Room Table	33
IV	Marriage To Second-Wife	45
V	Troubles	57
VI	The Missionary	65
VII	New Concepts	73
VIII	New Converts And New Troubles	83
IX	Soon-hee Is Pregnant	95
X	A Possible New Husband	109
XI	A New Chapel	123
XII	Wun-sik's First Church Service And Wun-yung's First Job	137
XIII	First-Wife's First Church Service	147
XIV	Wun-sik Proposes	157
XV	A Certain Satisfaction	167
XVI	A Church Wedding	179

Key To Pronunciation Of Korean Words

Though I studied with Seoul teachers, I am well aware that some will disagree with some of my pronunciations. However, I am tired of hearing the mispronunciation of other systems of romanization, and offer the following Korean sounds. I have avoided any special phonetic markings.

	IPA	Symbol In This book	Korean Koong-Moon
Broad **a** as in father, calm	a	ah*	아
Long **a** as in say, hay, ate	ei, e	ay	
Short **a** as in sang, hat	ae	ae	애
Long **e** as in see, key	i	ee	이
Short **e** as in ebb, met	e	e	에
Short **i** as in pit, if (Probably a trifle longer than our English short i)	I	i	
Broad **o** as broad, fought (Probably half way between aw and o)		aw*	오
Long **o** as in note, soul (Combination of u and oo as in Seoul)	o	o	
Short **u** as in cup, hut		u*	어
Long **u** as in flue, tube, boot	u	oo*	우
French **u** as in put, pull	u	eu	으
Lips rounded for **o** as in over, but saying **a** as in able		oe	

6

The **y** sound as in yes, you, often precedes the four vowels that are asterisked. They are then written
There are 15 ordinary consonantal sounds, using 10 letters: **k(g), n, t(d), r(l), m, p(b), s, -ng, ch(j), h.**
There are no initial g, d, b, j and l. However, when

pronounced
k	t	p	c h
g	d	b	j

occur between vowels, they are ;

The **g** is hard as in egg, get.
In a final position the **r** is pronounced l.
In a final position **-ng** is pronounced as in sing.
There are four aspirated consonants, **ch', k', t', p'**.
They are designated by an apostrophe after the romanized letter. Aspiration is simply a harder expulsion of breath than used for the ordinary consonants.
For the sake of getting closer to the true Korean pronunciation, I have hyphenated all multisyllable words.
Ordinary initial consonants are so soft (even the plosives **k, t, p, ch**) that they are many times misspelled in romanizing, i.e., Tae-goo becomes Dae-goo, when in fact the **t** has no vocalization.
There are also several diphthongs.

Note To Reader

My father, the Reverend Dr. James Edward Adams, lived from May 2, 1867, to June 25, 1929. He was the main apostolic church founder of the Protestant Christian faith in North and South Kyung-sahng Province, South Korea. Korean scholars gave him a Korean name, Ahn Euee-wah. Each syllable was a Chinese character or ideograph, as are all names in most of the Orient. This was the name that all Koreans knew him by during his missionary career of twenty-nine years.

Choosing the right characters, with appropriate and auspicious meanings, to accompany the owner all through life, was a very critical task. Ahn, meaning "peace," sounded somewhat like Adams. Euee-wah was the Korean attempt to say Edward and still fulfill the above requirement. The surname always comes first, thus Ahn Euee-wah. However, being a clergyman, all the Koreans called him Ahn Mawk-sah, which meant Pastor Adams.

During the years of my father's service, 1895 to 1921, the Christian Evangel was getting launched in the Tae-goo area. My father, known to most of the missionary community as Ned Adams, served as one of the itinerant pastors of many small, struggling church groups in the province. He also founded the Boys Academy, Kei-sung, which, together with Sinmyung Girls Academy, later developed into Kei-myung* University.

He and my mother, Nellie, made their home in Tae-goo, also spelled Taiku, Taegu and even Daegu. This became the base for his operations for the entire province.

As time went on, other medical, evangelistic, educational and agricultural missionaries joined the Tae-goo staff to help in the work.

Pastor Adams, or Ahn Mawk-sah, is the American Presbyterian missionary of this novel. The essential elements, however, are not fictitious but based on a true life experience. My two sisters and three brothers and I always eagerly awaited his return from visits to the country churches. We knew he'd have more stories like this one to tell us. All places and people, except mother and father and Pastor Lee Wun-yung have fictitious names. In actual life, however, Pastor Lee Wun-yung served the Presbyterian Church in Kyung-Ahn Presbytery, centered in Ahn-dawng, (Andong) 60 miles north of Tae-goo. I should also except Tawng-Sahn, or East-Mountain, where the missionary homes, hospital, Bible Institute, and missionary cemetery were and are located. The latter is where, among others, my mother Nellie's remains lie buried.

Due to failing health, father withdrew from mission-salaried support in 1921. However, he remained in Korea for a few more years under private support, and spear-headed the Forward Evangelistic Program that resulted in the addition of dozens upon dozens of healthy, new Christian communities.

My brother, the Rev. Dr. Edward Adams, was born February 6, 1895. He died September 7, 1965, after serving 42 years in Korea. He was also known to most of his occidental coworkers and friends as Ned Adams. He and his wife, Sue, spent many of these 42 years in Tae-goo, where in the course of time, Ned became one of the founders and the second president of Kei-myung University.

I must admit that since most of my adult-life in Korea was spent in Ahn-dawng, (Andong) I have used geographical features and village names from that area, and in my imagination woven them into this story, which actually took place in the Tae-goo area. Of course, Tae-goo is one of the larger cities of Korea. It is not an Eup, as this story portrays, but a Provincial Headquarters, the Province being North Kyung-sahng.

CHAPTER I
Kee-haw's Big Decision

Kee-haw sighed as he stretched out his full five-foot nine-inch frame on the fast-drying turf. Autumn was well underway in Korea. For Westerners the new century was still an infant. The sunset colors added an almost transparent glow to the dark red zelkova leaves over Kee-haw's head. Kee-haw spoke to his friend, resting beside him, "I'm 25 years old and not getting any younger. What do you do, Wun-sig-ee, when you've lived for ten years with a woman and still have no real affection for her?" Kee-haw sat up and continued, "The wedding was big and proper; she has borne me three fine boys, not to mention the girl, who must be of some value. But something is missing. There is no warm attachment, and a man needs something besides a woman to cook, carry water, and bear and raise him sons." Wun-sik had been born four months earlier than Kee-haw in this same little straw-thatched Korean village of Moo-jee-moo. They had grown up together, developing a warm comradeship through the years. Though their given names were Wun-sik and Kee-haw, since they were being such close friends they still called each other by the less formal, friendly forms of their childhood names, Wun-sig-ee and Kee-haw-yah.

Wun-sik too sat up, and looked at his friend of 25 years with considerable amazement. Wun-sik's eyes now popped questions, but he patiently held his peace. As he looked anew, Wun-sik saw that his friend, Kee-haw, was a little taller than most of the young men of his town, that he had a handsome face, with smooth, almost velvety skin and a nose a trifle more aquiline than that of most Koreans. And though he had recently shaved, one could see that the hair on his upper lip was rather sparse.

"You remember," Kee-haw went on, "how my honorable parents chose my wife for me when I was 15. They and the go-between worked out all the arrangements. My wife never saw my face and I never saw her eyes until after the wedding ceremony."

A remarkable warmth, reflecting the deep loyalty between the young men, shone from Wun-sik's dark eyes as he replied. "My friend, Kee-haw-yah, you know that the relation of husband and wife is one of the important Five Relations among men, as the scholar, Confucius, has ably set forth. For my part, I think that you have certainly done your best to fulfill your duty in this one." Wun-sik arose to his feet and continued, "No one can blame you if your wife has not responded with her part of this duty. Nor can they blame you if, over a period of ten years, you have grown weary in this relationship and take another wife."

Kee-haw interrupted at this point, "Wun-sig-ee, you may think that what I said in my deep emotion meant that I was contemplating divorce. Nothing could be further from the truth. Please don't ever repeat a word of this to another soul. My wife is hard enough to live with, without her hearing this and throwing it in my face. She keeps the house well and the children under as fair control as you could expect from a woman. And yet a man needs somewhat more than this — someone to share his hopes and manly ambitions, someone who calls him 'Lord-man' with her heart as well as her lips. Do you know what I mean, Wun-sig-ee?" Kee-haw held up both hands in his deep earnestness.

"I should say I do," Wun-sik answered empathetically, "for I have heard enough of Wun-yung's Mother's* nagging to wonder why you did not beat her before this. Tell me, my friend, if you care to, have you never really slapped her when she's been so impudent to you?"

"Oh, let's not spoil this wonderful hour with such sordid talk, Wun-sig-ee," Kee-haw parried and laughed.

Wun-sik sat down on the grass once more. The harvest was over. The rice was thrashed and sacked. Neither of them was in a hurry to do the odd jobs that had been saved for times like this. So for half an hour the men sat there resting, happy in each other's company. They watched the gold and scarlet zelkova leaves side-slip back and forth as they, too, came to rest nearby. Changing the subject, Wun-sik said, "Have you noticed, the pond is beginning to freeze around the edges? It's actually twelve years ago that you saved my life. Remember, freezing weather arrived earlier than usual that year and the irrigation pond above Moo-jee-moo had frozen over. The Honorable Teacher in the one-room School of the Classics was pretty kind. Can't you just see him pulling his beard several times, peering at the position of the sun and then in a generous gesture letting us all out of school early?

"Remember, we joined the preschool children who had been sliding on anything that had a smooth surface. Some even slid standing or squatting on their straw-shoes. A good run from the flat shore was all they needed to slide quite a distance on the slick ice of the pond. Some brought discarded lengths of old straw-rope and took turns, pulling each other across the ice.

"On that day when the old Teacher excused us before the regular time, the early freeze had moderated. A few warm days had even thawed the ice somewhat, particularly over the deepest part of the pond where the water still retained a little warmth. You and I, ignorant of the danger that lay ahead, arrived with the rest of the students and raced up to the pond. I arrived first, but you were close behind.

"The smaller children had been playing for quite awhile on the ice. Wearing our straw-shoes, both of us continued our race, weaving in and out among the smaller children, right across the ice, laughing and shouting. Oblivious to any thought of possible danger, our chase took us far out over the deepest part. Suddenly, amidst a few slight cracking sounds, I disappeared. Resurfacing quickly, I thrashed around, my padded clothes now sodden, adding to my weight. As I groped for the edge of the ice it kept breaking back, plunging me under the icy water.

"Remember, you had seen my predicament and stopped in time. While you instinctively knew your own danger, you could see me, a few feet ahead, fighting for life. What could you do? How could you save me? Quickly, you yelled, 'Help!' to the older children behind you. Then, without stopping to figure out why, you lay down flat, inching your way toward me. Your weight more evenly distributed, you quickly covered the ten or twelve feet to the edge of the hole. You grabbed my hands and kept my nose above the water. The other teenagers arrived soon, and one husky boy, following your example, lay down flat and wriggled forward till he could grab your ankles.

"The next two, standing on firm, solid ice, didn't have to lie down. Instead they grasped the first boy's ankles and began pulling back. Others, who had by now come up behind, formed two lines, putting their arms around the waists of those in front. Though the ice on the edge of the hole broke several more times, I was soon out of the icy water and running for home. Two of the boys who hadn't gotten wet ran with me, one on each side, holding my freezing hands and actually adding a little speed, for my soaked winter clothes slowed me down.

"This rescue happened nearly twelve years ago, yet I still remember the incident as though it took place yesterday. Though we seldom talk about it now, in the hearts of many here in our village, you are still the Moo-jee-moo hero. You know, Kee-haw, I often wonder if the time will ever come when I do something as brave and meaningful for you." Wun-sik had resumed his prostrate position on the grass during this recital of the near-tragic accident.

Suddenly, he sat up, saying, "To bargain for a second wife is no big matter. If you agree, I will save you the cost of a go-between and do it myself. Look here, Kee-haw-yah, every man, if he is a real man, has eyes in the front of his head. He notices when any attractive females are around. Confide in me. I know when to keep my mouth shut. Have you seen anyone who appeals?"

At this thought, Kee-haw sat up, too. He brightened immediately. His eyes gleamed as he answered Wun-sik. "You know, for over a year, in the back of my mind, I've been wondering and pondering and imagining what it would be like to have a second wife! I should have known that you, the friend of a lifetime, would have the answer to my innermost need. Have you seen Kim Saek-ssee* over near your home on the east side of town? She seems older than most of the other unmarried girls, which means she'll be closer to my age and probably more congenial."

Wun-sik broke in rather excitedly . . . "Do you mean the one they call Soon-hee, the miller's daughter?"

"Yes, she's the one," answered Kee-haw. "Wun-sig-ee, there is something that I think is even more important than her age. Every time I've caught glimpses of her, she's always been so cheerful. Waiting her turn with the other women at the well, invariably she's laughing gaily. And this is true with the other children in her parents' home. Wun-sig-ee, this is the spirit of joy, cheer, and happy, light-hearted living that I've missed for so many years," Kee-haw added.

"Yes, Kee-haw-yah, you're so right," Wun-sik replied. "I've seen that same quality and admired it. And since you're my best friend, I'll confess to you that in my dreamier moods I've often wondered what I would do if I were a little wealthier. Do you understand what I'm saying? I, too, have felt that she was the only one! You know, frankly, I wonder if there is any man in our village of Moo-jee-moo, young or old, who has not had similar dreams! You would do well to marry such as she. You can depend on me to drive the best bargain I ever have. After dinner I'll seek out her parents. I'll see you before too many days." The two men left each other and returned to their homes.

Kee-haw tried his best to work on some of the odd jobs around his place during the following week. But no matter what he did, he found his mind wandering down that twisty, narrow lane to the other side of town. How was Wun-sik-friend getting along? Why hadn't he come back sooner? At least he could have made a progress report! The suspense was dreadful.

Meanwhile, Wun-sik had kept his word to Kee-haw and sought out the parents that very evening. He approached them cautiously, knowing that to gain their consent would be no easy matter. Then the settlement of each detail of the marriage would have to follow. The entire process always required a veritable battle of wits. The old miller's crafty soul reveled in this. But fortunately for Kee-haw, Wun-sik put his finger on more than one facet that was slanted in Kee-haw's favor, and he didn't hesitate to make the most of them.

Kim-Miller, himself, who seemed to have a premonition of the purpose of the visit, was the quintessence of cordiality that first evening. "Come in, come in," he said expansively. He motioned Wun-sik to the hot-spot on the floor, almost over the kitchen fire.

The chill of the evening had not penetrated the room, so Wun-sik did his best to sit as far from the spot as possible. That is, of course, as far as was compatible with good taste and his host's delicate feelings. "You know you are most welcome," Kim-Miller began. "But I can't help but comment, Wun-sik-ssee,* that it's been such a very long time since I've seen you! When have we had a chance to just sit down and chat with each other? I really am terribly ashamed of myself, especially when we live so near each other. Please forgive me, Wun-sik-ssee. It was certainly not intentional," Kim apologized.

In a very few minutes, Kim's wife coughed outside the door of the sah-rahng, or men's sitting room. This announced her coming. The door jerked open and she set a tray with two cups of steaming amber-colored liquid on the floor. She placed them a little to one side of the doorway so she could step up into the room herself. Her voluminous, starched skirt rustled quite audibly as she entered. Kneeling on the floor, with hands placed in front of her, she softly gave the polite greeting: "Come quickly." The exact meaning of this phrase is lost in ancient times.

Then she offered each of the men a cup, serving Wun-sik first. The drink is one of the nicest that Korea has to offer. Several pinon pine-nuts floated on the surface. The drink itself was made from dried persimmons, soaked in very hot water and stirred until they are almost dissolved.

The two men conversed amiably for at least half an hour. Unhurriedly, they enjoyed their drinks. With the cups empty, both men felt that they had fulfilled all the requirements of the ancient rules of etiquette.

Wun-sik finally came to the point of his visit. "Kim-friend," he said, "you are indeed to be praised. You and your fine wife have done a superb job in raising that daughter of yours. She is such a happy person. You can tell this just by looking at her face, which, by the way, is **very** pleasant. How fortunate you two are!"

Kim-Miller's wife had left soon after serving the drinks. Wun-sik knew, however, that she was hovering nearby the paper door so as not to miss any of the conversation*. Of course she heard Kim-Miller's reply: "Thank-you, Wun-sik-friend, you are so observant! Needless to say, we are rather proud of our Soon-hee. To be very honest, she is quite a joy to us."

"You know, really, Kim-Miller," Wun-sik returned, "it's a little surprising that you haven't married her off long ago. It would be interesting to know if you have any good reason for this lapse. Not, you understand, that it makes any great difference."

"You are right, Wun-sik-ssee, we have erred; but she has always seemed so innocent and nice to have around. And she has really lived a very protected life in spite of her age, if you know what I mean. Actually, Wun-sik-friend, the normal time for marriage has only slipped by a trifle!"

"Yes, I am sure, Honorable Kim-Teacher*. I am also sure that the extra time at home under Kim-Lady's excellent tutelage more than compensates for the advanced age. You see, as you have doubtless surmised, I have come on behalf of my friend.

I am here to negotiate his marriage to your daughter. And it is possible that these seemingly minor details may be exceedingly important to some people! But tell me, please, about the dowry, and more about your charming daughter," Wun-sik replied.

Kim was more than well-prepared to elaborate on his daughter's delightful traits. But, being astute, he chose to parry, "Wun-sik-see, would you be so kind as to tell me which of your many friends you are speaking for?"

"Oh yes . . . of course . . . I should have told you sooner." He sat up as tall as he could stretch. "I am representing that worthy gentlemen, Paek Kee-haw*. Maybe I should say, 'He is my sponsor.' His character and standing in our community are well known. I'm sure I do not need to elaborate on them," Wun-sik concluded.

Kim knew that this was his time to shine. Very deliberately he tipped his cup to his lips to moisten his tongue with the few remaining drops. Wun-sik noticed that Kim did not bat an eye at the disclosure of who his daughter's suitor was. He would certainly have to be on the alert. Perhaps Kim was overconfident.

At any rate, Wun-sik marveled. For the next fifteen or twenty minutes, Kim scarcely paused to breathe as he narrated his daughter's wonderful accomplishments. Of course, not the least of these was her unfailing cheerfulness, which he illustrated, though it meant interrupting his list of praises, with the following story.

When she was thirteen years old, Soon-hee had accidentally broken the clay water-jar. This was the one she used to carry on her head the household water from the village well. When she got home, even though traces of tears were very much in evidence around both eyes, she was all smiles. She told how she had visited the village daem-jaeng-ee, or tinker, on the way home. She asked him to show her how to bore the holes for the metal staples. Then she borrowed his awl so that she could mend the water-jar herself.

18

Presenting her father with the mended pot, she finished her story saying, "Daddy, the tinker says that many times, people are more careful of their mended water-pot. They use it longer than before it was broken. And hah, hah! I had to laugh. The tinker said, 'Even if it begins to leak a year or two from now, if you use it for another purpose you can use it a lot longer.' Then he added, 'It will always stop leaking, too.' Hah, Hah, Hah! It was so funny, Daddy, I laughed and laughed, 'cause I knew what he meant. He was talking about the stuff that we save here at home. You know, the stuff you and Mommie carry out to the fields for fertilizer." Wun-sik couldn't help but laugh uproariously at this.

The evening passed rapidly, with Old-Man-Miller doing his best to keep the dowry agreement as low as possible. On the other hand, younger Wun-sik was dueling for every chance to score a point for Kee-haw.

The older man was wily all right, but still he was no match for Wun-sik. Just to be sure that he hadn't overlooked any detail, and also to give his friend Kee-haw the chance to get the best terms possible, Wun-sik didn't even return to the miller's house for six days. By then, the miller and his wife were doubtful that the deal had any chance of going through. They gave ground on some of the points much more easily.

On the seventh and eighth evenings, minor adjustments were made. In fact, the session on the eighth evening was quite short, and Wun-sik went across town to his friend's.

Kee-haw invited him into his sah-rahng, at the front of the house. Fortunately, it was away from the women's work area where the rest of the family members were busy or playing. Here they were comparatively free from interruptions or eavesdropping.

"Come in and sit over where the floor is warm," Kee-haw greeted him. "The evenings are beginning to get chilly." Then lowering his voice he continued, "I hope you've come with good news, Wun-sig-ee. I know I should not be impatient, but you have taken a very long time, don't you think? Did you run into any particular problem or difficulty?"

"Well," Wun-sik returned, "any time you push through a deal too quickly, you know as well as I, you're bound to lose somewhere. Any time you seem too anxious or hurried, the other fellow is going to do his best to take advantage of you. So after I broached the subject that first evening, I found out what kind of a dowry they were prepared to offer. Then I let the whole thing simmer until last night, when we agreed on most of the details. This evening it didn't take long to close the arrangement.

"You see, actually, her age was against her, even though you are happy that she's older than the other eligibles. But her age was in our favor. Then, too, her father, Kim-Miller, is really not as well off as you might suppose. Possibly the wife is not that thrifty. Anyway, this helped us a little, too, because the dowry was not quite up to norm."

Wun-sik winked at Kee-haw and dropping his voice to a mere whisper, he went on, "Most men don't want a girl that old; she's too set in her ways. So I made the most of it."

"Sh-h-h! Sh-h-h! You forget, every door is made of paper. Even here in the sah-rahng, the walls may have ears." Kee-haw stepped over to the door that opened onto the front stoop. He peered through the two-inch-square glass he'd inserted in it. All was clear.

Wun-sik continued, though even more softly, "As I mentioned, the family is poorer than you think. Old-Man-Kim has a pretty good business. But, I gathered from our dickering that they had to spend too much on the final illness of the old grandfather. My guess is, the reason she wasn't married off sooner is that the dowry was too small. Anyway, with these two rather important matters in our favor, Kim-Miller accepted the inevitable. Happy Soon-hee is to become your Second-Wife."

Kee-haw's eyes sparkled as he thanked his wonderful friend for his efforts, "Hah-nah-nim, the Honorable Lord of Heaven, has blessed us, Wun-sig-ee, in giving you a clever mind and tongue and in giving me a new lease on life. I just knew your efforts would meet with success, so I went ahead and actually gained several days' time. I spent them up on North Mountain.

I chose and cut some nice straight pine-trees for the corner posts, rafters, and door-frames of our new home!

"Of course, I'll have to build a one-kahn* room and lean-to-kitchen across on the other side of this courtyard, and the sooner I start, the faster the wood will dry and the less warping I'll get. I'd have gone crazy, sitting around home, wondering how you were getting along in your bargaining. So I also spent one day picking out and gathering quite a few big stones to use in the lower part of the walls. They are in the stream-bed several mah-jahng* up-stream.

"I don't think Sour-face has caught on yet; at least she doesn't seem suspicious, but I think I'll get started on the house tomorrow. Then, in very truth, all the demons of hell will break loose in my yard and home, and I'll be lucky if I escape in one piece."

"What time do you propose to start, Kee-haw-yah"? his friend asked. Both men were now speaking in the faintest of whispers.

"I'll go right to sleep as soon as you leave, and get up at the first cock's crow. The moon is old, so I'll have plenty of light to see my way up to my rock-piles," Kee-haw answered.

Wun-sik came right back with, "Look here, Kee-haw-yah, I've always enjoyed house-building. Let me help you build your love-nest. I know time lies heavy on our hands at this season of the year. We can set the wedding date a week or two earlier, if you finish the house sooner. Then, too, just my presence might change your anticipated typhoon to a mere spring shower. We will have fun working together. What do you say, Kee-haw-friend?"

"Oh Wun-sig-ee*, was there ever a friend like you? Am I not a lucky fellow?" Kee-haw exclaimed.

"You saved my life once. Maybe I can save yours now by bringing you happiness. I'll bring my oxcart over in the morning. With both of us working, we can hurry your dream to reality," Wun-sik winked again as he answered.

CHAPTER II
New House

The next morning, long before daylight, both oxcarts took off up the rough, dirt road that paralleled the stream. Kee-haw had thoughtfully detoured the town to avoid waking the other villagers. Few houses showed any lights. Not many people were awake at this hour in Moo-jee-moo. Fortunately Kee-haw's home was on the north edge of town. Kee-haw and Wun-sik waited until they were out of earshot. Then, knowing that no one could possibly hear them, they continued their conversation of the previous night. They had to raise their voices above the squealing axles and the grinding of rocks under the wheels.

"This is much better than having to whisper all the time, huh!" Kee-haw, who was in front, called back.

"Yeah, even the birds aren't listening this early," Wun-sik hollered. "Isn't it grand, being kings for an hour or two with nobody to say us nay!"

"Wun-sig-ee, do you think I'll ever be King in my own house? You know everyone says that these dual-wife homes have more headaches than a dog's belly has fleas. What would be your answer to that?"

"I'd say it's a little late to be taken in by that kind of gossip," Wun-sik shot back. "There's nothing new about such marriages. They're as old as the hills on each side of us, Kee-haw-friend! We've surely gotten a good start this morning. We'll have three hours of the hardest, backbreaking work finished by breakfast time. Then we'll face your hellion-wife. I just hope she doesn't put any poison in our rice."

Kee-haw had already asked Wun-sik the night before to eat his meals at their home. After all, this was but a small gesture by which to show his appreciation for all those long hours of fatigue. Now Kee-haw, appreciating his friend's latest humor, threw back his head and let out a great whoop of laughter!

The moon touched the tops of the tallest pines on the ridge to the left. The dark blue of the night sky was beginning to lighten on their right. The bumpy road gradually drew closer to the stream-bed, until their right wheels entered the water. Occasionally a frightened fish splashed farther out in the dark middle of the stream. The ox and the cow kept slogging along, sometimes in little side-eddies, sometimes on dry land.

As the day broke and shadows took on forms, Kee-haw was at last rewarded by seeing his rock-piles up ahead. The lead-cow recognizing them, too, drew abreast and stopped. Because huge boulders were strewn everywhere, there was no good place to turn the carts around. The two men had no choice but to unhitch both animals and together swing the heavy wagons around by hand. When the faithful beasts were rehitched, the two-wheeled carts were flat for loading.

The men made a rough rectangle of fairly flat rocks on the perimeters of the cart-beds. This would keep the rounder rocks which they piled inside the outline from rolling off on the way home. Then they loaded on the rest of the rocks, pyramiding them up.

During the hour or more of the loading, both men enjoyed the opportunity to talk to their hearts' content. The prospects of the days ahead were the main subjects. Kee-haw averred that a man should be fair and firm, not only in his dealings with each member of his family, but with others. If he were, no untoward or impossible situations could develop that time would not heal.

He did acknowledge that this house-building might take an extra amount of patience and fortitude. But this was because it was being built under the scrutiny of First-Wife's angry eyes. "However," he concluded, "your presence is the best thing that could have happened under the circumstances. As you said, it can't help but mitigate the typhoon! How can I ever thank you enough?"

Wun-sik glowed under his friend's praise. He felt happy to be able to help him. Yet he knew full well that every word was true and also that Kee-haw would have done the same for him, had circumstances been reversed. Aloud he said, "Is there anything in this world more beautiful than a man's clean, loyal feeling for his friend?"

By now the sun had almost topped the eastern ridge of the mountain. The early vivid pinks paled to a pastel saffron, streaked ever so gently with azure. The trip back down took much longer than they had anticipated. The sturdy wagons were heavily loaded. To protect the wheels from damage, many times both men had to ease one over a particularly large rock in the roadbed. The ox and cow strained their withers against the yokes, as the two strong men grasped and turned the heavy spokes of one of the large wheels. What tremendous feats could be accomplished with this remarkable combination!

At last, sweaty and extremely tired and dirty, the little cavalcade pulled into Kee-haw's courtyard. The last breakfast dish had been washed and put away an hour before. Kee-haw quickly went around behind the house and dragged out an old, partly broken, baked clay-pot. He scrubbed and rinsed it off. Very carefully and evenly he divided up the steaming-hot, porridge-like chook for the ox and the cow.

Before leaving in the pre-dawn, he had very quietly put an extra measure of barley in the cow's chook-cauldron*. He knew that the family would not notice the difference, but would build and stoke the fire under it.

Then Kee-haw got the wash-basin which was hanging on a nail on the inside of the kitchen door post and, using the gourd-dipper, filled it with water from the Ali Baba-sized jar which stood just inside the outside kitchen-door. Carrying the basin with the dipper floating on the water, he invited Wun-sik to follow and went across to the far side of the courtyard. There they removed their cotton jackets and with a lot of blowing and splashing scrubbed down from the waist up.

By the time they were ready, enough rice for both had been warmed and served up. Each man had an extra dish of kim-chee* and some hot soup. Wun-sik noted with new appreciation how provident and resourceful Wun-yung's Mother was as she went about meeting this major emergency. Suddenly she had to dish up food for twice the number she had expected! This was very close to an act of magic. Kee-haw couldn't help but notice it, too, though rather grudgingly.

Both of them took note that her face was not a happy one, and slowly nodded at each other. Yet, she was cool, efficient and quiet. They couldn't help but admire these qualities. Even the children, and particularly Wun-yung, the eldest son, pitched right in and helped without being asked. All helped in many ways. And the daughter, Sayt-jjae, meaning Third, who appeared to be about five or six, seemed to be everywhere at once. She was helping her mother whenever possible and picking up after the boys. Her sweet little face was clean and bright. In contrast to her mother, she looked almost angelic in her short pink jacket, radiating joy as she flew back and forth.

None of these amenities was lost on Wun-sik. He quickly recalled the gist of Kee-haw's tribute, "She keeps a nice house and has done well by the children." Wistfully he thought, "What a pity her temperament doesn't match her other fine qualities."

During breakfast, Wun-yung's Mother wasn't as vocal as usual. The two men glanced at each other knowingly. So far their hopes had been realized! As they ate in the family/living/bedroom next to the bi-level kitchen, they could hear her slight steady muttering. And before breakfast was over, they agreed that the atmosphere was somewhat frigid.

The two friends worked hard that day and the next. They used most of the stones that their two wagons had hauled down from the stream-bed. The lower walls of the small cottage and lean-to were taking shape. This year's monsoon season was clearly a thing of the past, so the two friends talked it over. They decided that it might be easier to install the awn-dawl*, or radiant-heat floor, first. The wooden posts and wattle of the upper walls could be erected afterward.

So on the third day they again got an early start and took the ox and cow and both carts, though neither would have to be loaded as heavily as on the first morning. No round stones could be used in this operation. They had to go much farther up the mountain valley. Of course the road was even worse. Fortunately, the flat, awn-dawl stones they needed would not slip as easily on the beds of the wagons. They wouldn't have to be as careful in loading them. But they were wider, which made them break more easily. So they still had to exercise a good deal of care.

The only negative incident during the trip occurred when one of the large wooden spokes in Wun-sik's right wagon-wheel loosened. This was serious business, especially with such a load. One loose spoke could easily lead to another, causing the whole wheel to go to pieces in a very short time, if it weren't well repaired.

If the wheel were only off the wagon, it wouldn't be hard to fix, at least temporarily. Both wagons came to a quick halt and Kee-haw expressed both their feelings with an extra loud, "Ah-ee-gaw*!" They talked it over. Wun-sik said: "I'm afraid, Kee-haw-yah, our luck has turned against us. There must be some nasty taw-ggae-bee* around, having a good time at our expense."

Kee-haw interjected, "Right! And the worst of it is, one never knows how to handle those little rascals. If we take my wagon on down to Moo-jee-moo to get some better tools to fix yours with, those rascals could do more damage while we're gone! So maybe we'd just better do the best we can with the tools we have with us. What do you say, Wun-sig-ee?"

"You were telling me recently about the time you encountered a similar problem with a much lighter load," Wun-sik responded. "Don't you have the same tools in that box of yours that you had then?"

"To tell you the truth, I do," Kee-haw answered. "If you agree, let's just tough it out right here and maybe even save a few hours' time. First, let's pile up some rocks under this right side of your wagon. Then we'll have to chop a long pole for a lever. We'll have that wheel off in no time."

Rocks lay everywhere, so it didn't take long to pile several flat ones under the right side of Wun-sik's crippled wagon. While Wun-sik was finishing that job, Kee-haw climbed up the mountain-side, looking for a pole long enough to pry up that side of the wagon.

They were close to Moo-jee-moo by now, and the woodcutters had cleaned up all the dead wood. Kee-haw went back to his wagon and got his axe, which he always carried in the tool box when on some errand away from home. Choosing a spot where the living pines were thick, he quickly toppled a medium-sized one. He cut the trunk very close to the ground, so he wouldn't waste any of the precious wood, and deftly stripped the branches, tying them in two bundles with both ends of his spare rope; then he threw them on the wagon.

Wun-sik had finished his job and had an extra large flat stone ready to slip into place when the wagon went up. But the wagon didn't go up, even though both men got their shoulders under the pole and "yung-chig-eed*" together. The load of awn-dawl won the day!

"It's tough, Wun-sig-ee, but we'll just have to unload this side of your wagon!" Kee-haw exploded, with another big "Ah-ee-gaw*."

Reluctantly they started in. With both of them working together, it only took fifteen or twenty minutes to unload the right half. Again they pried with the pole, and this time Kee-haw could hold it alone, while Wun-sik slipped the final rock into place. They removed the long square pin that held the wheel on the axle.

Off came the wheel! While Kee-haw had been cutting and trimming the pole. Wun-sik had taken the sickle and whittled several long, thick oak-wood wedges.

Carefully, they removed the metal rim. Then with the blunt back of the axe, they hammered the shims down into place around the butt end of the offending spoke, right where it came through the wooden rim. "Kee-haw-yah," Wun-sik shrieked, and punctuated it by dancing a little caper, "we couldn't have done it better, if we'd been doing it at home!"

By the time they arrived at home and unloaded the two carts, it was considerably past noon. The energy from their impromptu lunches was gone. Both men needed a good noonday meal.

The two older children wouldn't return from school for two more hours. Third was playing with some friends at a neighbor's home, and the youngest son was already napping.

Wun-yung's Mother brought the two little one-person tables, loaded with simple food, in to the two men. She was noticeably awkward, not even trying to be polite. Roughly, she placed a table in front of each man.

With the children out of earshot, she began through clenched teeth: "I don't know why I'm doing this! I really ought to poison every dish on here! Is there to be no peace under our roof? What have I done that is so wrong to deserve this?"

Kee-haw replied a little sheepishly: "Now look here, Wun-yung's Mom, you're in the presence of our guest. This is no time or place for such talk! You have done so well so far; why this explosion now? You should be happy to have a strong, young back to help with the heavy housework." Wun-yung's Mother dabbed at her eyes with her apron and backed out of the door, down into the kitchen.

Following the meal, Kee-haw himself had to go out the front door of the living room. He put on his shoes, went around the house and down onto the earthen floor of the kitchen. He dipped two bowls of hot rice-flavored water* out of the big cauldron, for his friend and himself.

After they had finished drinking and eating and rinsing their teeth, Wun-sik blurted out, "This is the worse possible timing, Kee-haw, I know. But during the last few days, things have gotten rather badly out of control at my house. I promised the Inside Person* to come back and tend to them this afternoon. But I also know that we have an awful long way to go on the new house across there, including the very heavy work of laying those big awn-dawl. That makes my leaving now, even though for only a few hours, all the more thoughtless and hard on you, I know. I'll try also to get a few things done ahead of time at home. Then we won't have to break in again on our work here for awhile. Please, please forgive the discourtesy of leaving you now." Kee-haw's immediate response to his friend was, "Don't worry. I'll do the jobs that a single fellow can do and wait for your return to do the rest."

Wun-sik backed out the door and down off the porch into his shoes on the stoop. He turned his ox and cart around and headed for home. Kee-haw then thought to himself, "Now what lies ahead of me this afternoon? With no one else around, what course will Sour-face choose as her method of attack? Is there anything that I can do to protect myself and my love-nest-in-the-making?" Try as he would, no very acceptable plan came to mind. This much he knew: the children would be back from school shortly after four o'clock. Therefore, whatever she did would have to be in the next couple of hours.

Kee-haw proceeded to mix some more heavy clay-mud and cut up some rather coarse rice-straw to scatter over and mix in it. Then he took off his shoes and homemade socks and rolled up his trousers so he could tramp the mixture. This worked well and his feet were tough enough that the coarse straw didn't lacerate them.

He would have the small rice-cauldron for the two of them hung next to the bedroom wall and right at the midpoint. Then he would build the piers under the awn-dawl floor so that the flues radiated out from the cauldron like the ribs of a fan. This would carry the warm air and smoke underneath to even the farthest part of the room. Finally, he would gather the flues together to take the smoke out the clay pipe in the center of the far side.

Somehow he must keep the heated air and smoke from rushing through the central flues to the chimney, a fact which would of course, leave the rest of the room cold. He determined to make these central flues the narrowest. Then he would gradually increase the flue widths, as they got farther and farther from the center. When he got through, he would boast of the best heated floor in the village, if not the county!

This afternoon, if everything went well, he might finish the first row of piers at the kitchen end of the room and even get a few awn-dawl laid on them. Fortunately, they had allowed for some breakage on the way home, by cutting out and bringing a few extra awn-dawl.

He looked around. Sure enough, there were more damaged awn-dawl than he expected. But then again, he needed more stones in the piers than they had brought on the first trip. So he would be able to use most of the extras. It might even save him another short trip to the mountain.

These and other thoughts and plans went through his head, as he worked away. For over an hour, through his well-made plans and steady work, he made good progress on the basic walls and piers. He even got one heavy awn-dawl in place, spanning the space between two of the central piers. He smiled to himself. Now, if only Sour-face will behave herself.

CHAPTER III
Weapon: The Dining Room Table

At that precise moment, the outdoor kitchen door swung wide open, and the lady in question emerged. As though she had read his thoughts, she said: "Loving husband, the fresh kim-chee is all gone, so also is the Chinese cabbage we make it with. The baby's alone and I'm busy with several other things anyway. Would you be so useful as to go out to the garden and pull a couple of heads of cabbage. It's somewhat out of your way, but if you'd go around by the stream on the way back, it would be a big help. It'll take only a few minutes to wash the dirt off the roots and would save a lot of our precious village well water."

He grunted an incomprehensible answer, as men of every nation occasionally do. Thinking, "While I wash the roots, I'll also wash my legs and save some more water," he grabbed a haw-mee* and left. He hoped, as he walked toward the garden, that this was a real emergency and not just the first of many chores she would think up for him to do throughout the afternoon.

In record time, he was back with two large, clean heads of cabbage. He complimented himself on how lucky he was that the task was over so soon. She heard him coming and met him at the door, large, sharp, kitchen cleaver-knife in hand. No grateful smile broke her somber, solemn face, nor any clear word of gratitude. Instead, she spoke only the one word: "Good." She shut the door, and he listened to her receding footsteps.

He realized that he would have to be near, working with the mud-mortar most of the time. So he went to the ox-lean-to on the other side of the old house, where he pulled down a very old pair of straw-shoes which he had saved for just such an occasion. He wouldn't even put his socks back on. No use giving Sour-face more work than usual to complain about.

Back he went to his mud-pile. "And anyway," he thought, "before too long, Sweet Soon-hee* will be taking care of most of my personal needs. Oh-h-h! If I could only skip the next two or three weeks!" Softly he said her name again, this time out loud, just to hear what it sounded like, "Sweet Soon-hee." Whoever would have thought that a name could have so much meaning in it, be so lovely and fit a person so perfectly. Sweet and docile! Could any man ask for more?

"SWEET SOON-HEE!" a screeching voice shouted right in his ears. He had forgotten that he was making so much noise, slapping the mud-mortar into the cracks of the rising piers. A thunderstorm could have crept up on him without his even suspecting it! In fact, in a sense, one had. Sour-face now knew who his bride-to-be was! What a calamity! He threw up his hands in utter despair and inadvertently threw several specks of mud right into her face.

"So this is the way you're going to treat me from now on!" she shrieked at the top of her voice. "Throwing mud in my face! I don't care who hears me! You're a dirty, foul, mud-slinging philanderer! Take your hussy and go away! Go away anywhere! Just don't stay near me and my children, faithless husband!"

She swooped up several handsful of mud and threw them at the white work-pants that so far he'd kept fairly clean. "Tell her this is my wedding present to you, you ingrate!" Her voice was beginning to break and taper down as she wiped her hands on the few remaining clean places on his pants.

"I just hope somebody comes by this afternoon, sees your pants and tells all of Moo-jee-moo how clumsy you are. Do you mean to tell me that after all the time you've wasted from the many things we need done around the house you only have one awn-dawl in place? And look, it isn't even level or solid." She leaned heavily on one exposed corner, exerting enough leverage to pull it loose. In the process it also dislodged several other stones on top of one pier. This dropped the heavy awn-dawl down into the flue between.

Kee-haw knew full well that if only he had finished all the piers first, this could never have happened. At least, not without a sledge-hammer. He also knew that Sour-face was out to make trouble and to delay and discourage the building process as much as possible. "Anyway," he mused to himself, "she didn't do it behind my back, if that is any comfort."

Deep in his heart, Kee-haw also knew that she had been faithful to him and the family. And **she** had kept her womanly trait of gossiping to a minimum. After all, a man couldn't ask for much more than that! As for the muddy trousers, she was the one who would suffer the most. By the wildest stretch of the imagination, she would never throw away a pair that had so much wear left in them. And she would have to beat them on one of the laundry rocks to get them clean enough even to use them as work-pants.

So he simply gritted his teeth and glared as she retreated to the kitchen. Perhaps Wun-sik's presence on the other days would keep her temper under control. No one would believe him if he told them what had just happened. His silence, therefore, would simply be part of that "extra amount of patience and fortitude" that he'd told Wun-sik it would take.

That afternoon, after school, Wun-yung kept calling to his younger brother and sister, "Why are both of you so slow? Don't you know that our Honorable Dad and Naw Teacher are building a new house right in our yard? Come on! Let's run. I'll promise not to run too fast for you."

"That's right," yelled Tool-jjae, "let's see if we can run all the way home without stopping once."

In a few minutes the three children raced into their yard, flushed with excitement about the new house. Kee-haw thought to himself, "Ah-ee-gaw*, now I'll have some freedom for the rest of the afternoon."

Kee-haw had already replaced the one awn-dawl. In greeting Wun-yung he said, "Son, you know my friend, Wun-sik-ssee. He's a wonderful fellow. He helped me this morning and into the afternoon. And he's going to help me again tomorrow. I hope you don't mind working with us Saturday afternoon and Sunday."

Wun-yung was ten, Korean count*, and rather husky for his age. After being cooped up in school, he was glad to carry any amount of rocks and mud for his father.

"Of course not, Honorable Dad. Really, it's lots of fun, helping you. I never knew how hard it was to build a house, and I'm certainly learning a lot, even during play-time," Wun-yung answered.

With Wun-yung's help, the work went faster and didn't halt until after sundown and the call for dinner. In fact, they were able to complete the entire first row of awn-dawl along the western kitchen-side of the room. So, proud of what they had accomplished together, Kee-haw and Wun-yung chatted happily as they washed their hands and feet.

"Honorable Dad, are you expecting more guests than before?" Wun-yung began. "Is that why you're building a guest-house?" he asked.

"Well, not exactly," Kee-haw parried. "To be very honest with you, son, we're expecting an addition to the family."

"You mean another baby? But he won't need a whole house, not yet anyway!"

"No, not a baby, son. We have plenty of children right now. This will be like another mother, but a little younger; and, sh-h-h, don't mention this to anyone, but maybe a little kinder. Thanks again for your help today, son. Someday maybe you'll realize how very much it means to me. Now run on in to dinner. Remember, 'Mum's the word,' " and Kee-haw held his finger up to his lips and then patted Wun-yung's shoulder. "If you need any help tonight on your homework, let me know."

Kee-haw soon followed him in very quietly, and in a dark corner of the living/dining/bedroom, changed to a light pair of long underpants for the evening. The room was quite warm, and no guests were expected. His work-pants were so dirty that he'd left them in the cow-shed.

Dinner passed quite smoothly, considering the tensions. The pressures of the afternoon seemed to have been spent, and peace prevailed that evening. Kee-haw played with the baby for awhile. This relieved Wun-yung's Mother from carrying him on her back while she tidied up the kitchen. Middle Son, now eight, whom they usually called Tool-jjae, meaning Second, busied himself with his homework. Sayt-jjae, which meant Third, soon finished her job, helping Wun-yung's Mother dry the dishes. She then joined the fun on the living room floor. Wun-yung's Mother stayed in the kitchen much longer than usual. Baby-brother soon gave up the fight to keep his eyes open. He put his thumb in his mouth. Then he curled up on the warm floor and went to sleep.

Kee-haw, after working hard from long before sunrise till after sunset for three days, decided he would rest and read for awhile. Sayt-jjae and Middle Son found something that intrigued them both. And Wun-yung was still engrossed in his homework.

Kee-haw's eyes soon grew heavy. Luckily, he remembered that he hadn't fed the work-cow, so he lit the spare, small, round-wicked oil-lamp and went on through the kitchen. That was the shortest way, as the cow lean-to was built against one wall of the kitchen.

The patiently waiting cow gave Kee-haw a short welcoming bellow. Kee-haw answered, "Sorry, old girl, I'll have it here in a hurry." He carried the mended crock back into the kitchen and dipped out the chook from the cow's cauldron. Then he brought it back to the lean-to and placed it near the back wall. There the cow could eat without stepping on the crock and breaking it again.

In the meantime, Wun-yung's Mother had gone up the two steps into the living room.

Kee-haw shut the wooden bolt on the inside of the outer kitchen door. After checking the other outside doors, he retired to the sah-rahng. On his way, as he passed the living room, he stuck his head in to be sure that Wun-yung did not need him. Then he sank exhausted onto the warm sah-rahng floor, pulled a quilt over himself and fell asleep.

Before dawn the next morning, Kee-haw awoke to the sound of rain dripping from the eaves. Fortunately, it was not a summer-monsoon, drenching rain, but a soft, gentle, fall rain. Maybe it had not damaged the fresh awn-dawl or part of an awn-dawl as yet. He had no time to waste. The diffused light from the old last-quarter moon would offer as much help as he needed. Day was beginning to break.

Quickly he found his old shoes under the front porch, ran round to the ox-shed and located several empty straw rice-bags. With his knife he quickly opened several of them. Then he sloshed over to the one-kahn room, or as much as there was of it. Hurriedly he laid a row of the opened, spread-out sacks over the strip of finished awn-dawl. This he figured would protect that precious row from the rain.

Cold and wet from head to toe, he hurriedly rubbed down and changed into his dirty but dry trousers. Meanwhile, Wun-yung's Mother had heated up some soup left from the day before, and Kee-haw quaffed it noisily, to the tune of many burps of satisfaction and hearty contentment. The partly done awn-dawl was safe, at least if it didn't rain long!

After the children's breakfast, Kee-haw gave Middle Son the better of two oil-paper umbrellas to carry to school. Sayt-jjae could go with him. Wun-yung made do with the badly torn and patched older one. When the children were gone and before Kee-haw had gotten halfway through his own breakfast, Wun-yung's Mother began her tirade. She unleashed the cutting, scathing, vitriolic vituperation for which she was famous. None was her better!!

She was down in the kitchen, but the paper-covered lattice-door was not in the least sound-proof. She knew that Kee-haw heard every word that she uttered. "Aren't **I** producing enough children to carry on **your** family name, so that you have to add another woman to our crowded house?" she screamed.

"Or is it that you're just tired of my cooking, and somebody's told you that a new wife would cook you new gourmet dishes?"

Kee-haw had tried to answer her when she boiled over on previous occasions. But he knew that he would have trouble making himself heard. So instead of trying, he just quietly finished his breakfast.

The umbrellas were both gone, and there was little chance of friend Wun-sik turning up on a day like this. Kee-haw decided to go out to the cow-shed to find something he could mend or do. Let Sour-face keep up her screaming. Poor little Baby-brother was probably used to it. He would be the only sufferer!

Kee-haw did not carry his small table with its empty dishes to the kitchen door, as was his usual, thoughtful habit. Instead he noiselessly slipped outdoors and into his old shoes. He would keep away from her as much as possible!

As he went around to the shed, the sight of the cow reminded him that his hungry animal's needs had been forgotten. He chided himself mentally, "Just because you're having a bad time doesn't mean that you have to drag the rest of the world with you, Kee-haw, you thoughtless rogue." He picked up the feed-crock and gave the cow a pat on the rump. "I'll be right back, old girl," he said, and hurried to the kitchen and the cauldron of hot chook.

Just as he stepped from the yard into the kitchen, his wife came down the two steps opposite from the living room. She was holding his breakfast table in both hands. He could see that she was livid with rage. "So now the Lord-man has become so elevated, he can't even bring his table to the kitchen-door!" she screamed. Then, with her full strength, she hurled the table, dishes, unfinished soup, and chili-pepper sauce right at his face. He had turned toward the ox-cauldron, and her outburst caught him unaware. One partly cracked dish broke, and the sharp edge gashed his temple, just above the outer corner of his left eye.

Blood streamed down his face and onto his everyday, white work-jacket. Some of it splashed below the jacket, making a beautiful tri-colored contrast on his yellowish-brown-spotted white trousers. The blood which missed both jacket and trousers made the hard-packed, clay floor slippery and dangerous. He quickly grabbed an old rag and wiped the floor clean. Then holding the rag and his hands under his chin, he headed for the big water jar and the basin, over by the outside door.

Wun-yung's Mother screamed after him, "Too bad I didn't kill you, you useless, faithless dog!"

While trying both to clean his face and hands of the excess blood and to staunch the flow, Kee-haw had stepped outdoors, and he suddenly realized he wasn't really getting very wet. Sure enough, the rain was beginning to let up. After folding a nice, clean, white cloth he had found in the sah-rahng, he tied it in place over the wound with a longer rag that wasn't as clean. He finished feeding the cow and went back to work, muttering to himself, "Well, I suppose it could have been worse!"

Kee-haw was happy to learn that the rain hadn't soaked far into the partly-built but exposed piers. He took his short-handled hoe, or haw-mee, and quickly scraped off the slushy exteriors. This would stop the moisture from soaking in any farther. Then he began to mix a new batch of mud-mortar opposite where he'd be using it today. Bringing over the small pile of much too wet left-over mortar from yesterday, he mixed it in with the new. This saved carrying a lot of water.

He paused to take the rice-bags off the awn-dawl that he'd finished yesterday. As he did this another happy thought occurred! "I wonder if it's possible that there are good spirits as well as the bad and mischievous ones we've always known existed. I mean spirits that actually help people in need. On the surface, anyone might say that I came off the worse in that encounter awhile ago. But if it counts for anything, I didn't lose my temper and beat up on her. And I could very easily have done that without incurring the blame of anyone!

"Yet, is it possible that I am a sissy, just to stand and take it? Maybe, but more likely there is some sort of good spirit somewhere that's helping me to actually win this battle of wits. Whatever the case, this business of taking a second wife seems to be stirring up an evil spirit! Maybe it's better not to give this evil spirit any more chance to work against me."

By now he had finished taking the rice-sacks off the single row of awn-dawl. He was elated to see that the mud-mortar he had used in the piers yesterday was in such good condition. Thanks to the light rain and the straw-bags, he wouldn't have to sprinkle the outer edges before adding another row of awn-dawl. He smiled again, murmuring to himself, "That 'good spirit' has certainly been on the job."

A shadow crossed the ground in front of him and a familiar voice said: "What good spirit? Are you completely crazy, with that filthy rag around your head and this funny talk about spirits?"

Kee-haw recognized the voice of his friend. He grinned broadly as he grabbed one hand and whacked him on the shoulder with his clean elbow. He lowered his voice: "Wun-sig-ee," he said, "you won't believe it, but it's the truth just the same. An evil spirit hit me on the head, but a good spirit has been bringing me lots of luck. And the best luck is your coming right now. Remember, Confucius said, 'One joy dispels a hundred cares.' Wun-sig-ee, look at how much Wun-yung and I got done yesterday! Even without you here.

"You're a real friend to come out in such weather, though I guess it's clearing up now. Come on, we can talk while we work. Do you want to tramp the mud-mortar this time, or shall I?"

"Say, Kee-haw, I can't tell you how much it means to me to see you in such good spirits. I was really afraid, being away most of yesterday afternoon, and again for several hours this morning. You could have had some serious trouble. In fact I didn't know what to expect as I came this morning. But you've made good progress in spite of the rain! Congratulations!" Wun-sik continued. "Sure, I'll be glad to tramp the mud, if you want me to. But to tell you the truth, it'd be a lot faster if both of us did it. Have you got any clay dug up that we can use now?"

"Yes, plenty more. We only used a small part of what I dug up yesterday. And it didn't rain enough to pack it down again. You see, that's what I was saying when you arrived; 'Some good spirit must be on our side!' "

Wun-sik said, "Yes, I understand, but tell me what happened to your head." And Kee-haw answered, "Please, let's not talk about that now."

By this time they were both working hard and joshing each other back and forth. After mixing the new supply of mortar, both went to work on the piers and awn-dawl. By lunchtime, they had finished three-quarters of another row.

Lunch was a bit dull, since the friends were not able to talk about anything but weather and stale community gossip. Wun-yung's Mother did everything properly, came and went, but said nothing. After lunch, each man smoked a very small pinch of tobacco in the tiny bowl of his long-stemmed pipe. They went back to work, relaxed and jovial.

Of course, Wun-sik was very curious. But he waited until they were on the third row of awn-dawl. By then he was able to muster enough courage to ask Kee-haw what happened to the other fellow!

Kee-haw's jovial mood had not diminished one whit and he played right up to the banter. "Oh! the other guy couldn't even stand on his two feet when I finished with him!

"But seriously, Wun-sig-ee, you know that in our country throwing a table loaded with dishes and what not at a person is the worst possible insult. Yet that's what happened to me. Really, you should have been here to see it."

Then in an undertone, Kee-haw added, "But maybe it's just as well that you weren't. You see, Wun-sik-friend, it gave Sour-face a chance to get some of the poison out of her system. And now, when she sees she's outnumbered and we're going right ahead, maybe things will go a little smoother.

"At least, Wun-sig-ee, I didn't do anything intentionally to provoke her further and make matters worse. So maybe, now remember I said 'maybe,' there's some blue sky ahead."

"I thought I was your bosom friend," Wun-sik replied, "but you won't even tell me how it happened. Are you ashamed of it? Isn't it an honorable wound?" They were still speaking in an undertone.

"Oh my! Do I have to defend my wounds to my friend? Can't I even enjoy them by myself?" A flash of anger lit up Kee-haw's eyes, but not for long. "No, no, I take it back! I don't know why I have relished keeping you in the dark. Maybe it's human nature to like a secret, but there's really no reason for your not knowing, Wun-sik-friend."

With his voice scarcely above a whisper, Kee-haw related the details of the three incidents and how he had responded or failed to react.

When he had finished, Wun-sik complimented him by saying, "My friend, where did you get this saintliness? I am sure that I, and ninety percent of the rest of Korean men, would not have exercised as much restraint as you did. It makes me very proud to be your friend!"

With Wun-sik's help, Kee-haw was able to finish the cottage in four and a half weeks. He had gotten the rice-straw-thatched roof on early, so they could work indoors whenever it rained. Gradually he moved most of his personal belongings into it. The main room was the standard one-kahn, approximately eight feet square. It looked very trim and neat with its fresh, heavy oil-paper floor. The mud walls were drying fast and the paper-pasted-on-wires ceiling didn't have a single fly-speck on it.

He had included a high closet on one wall, protruding out under the eaves, so it was properly protected from the weather. The springless mattress and the winter quilts could be kept there in the daytime, making more space available in the room.

In some ways it was nicer than many Korean living/dining/sleeping rooms. He and his friend had added a sturdy porch on the front. Kee-haw wondered whether his new bride would notice all these niceties. Yes, she was to be his ch'up, his Second-Wife, but he would surely help her to forget this inferiority in their new joy.

CHAPTER IV
Marriage To Second Wife

During the last week of this house-building, Kee-haw had hired the best seamstress in Moo-jee-moo to help Wun-sik's wife make some new wedding clothes for him. Though Wun-sik's wife had already started work on this project, Kee-haw insisted that she have help.

Needless to say, Kim-Miller's household was even more astir with wedding preparations. Soon-hee and her mother worked day and night preparing the clothes and other items yet missing from the paraphernalia of the trousseau. Poor Kim-Miller had to visit several of his more well-to-do clients and arrange advances on their next year's milling bills, to cover the items of the contracted dowry. And Wun-sik was always clearing his throat* outside the miller's Great-Gate, dropping by to make sure that everything was being done as agreed.

Just to be sure of a favorable horoscope, Kee-haw had some time previously sent his sah-joo, or four pillars, to the bride-elect's family. These four pillars consisted of the year, month, day and hour of his birth. Kim-Miller had then sent it with Soon-hee's sah-joo to the Moo-jee-moo sorceress.

When Kee-haw and Wun-sik knew approximately how soon the cottage would be dry and ready for occupancy, they also relayed this information on to the village sorceress. She in turn then fixed the lucky date for the wedding.

Though Kee-haw for many years had been forced by circumstances to be rather frugal, he suddenly became unusually generous. Several weeks before, he had asked Wun-sik to deliver gifts of silk and cotton piece-goods to the Kims' home. He also gave Soon-hee an unusually large hairpin, worn only by married women. It was of the best quality gold, half an inch thick and four or five inches long. At one end it had a beautifully wrought dragon-head.

Though not always wrought of gold, a silver pin was typical female jewelry in this Land of the Morning Calm*, and many times was a real luxury.

Now that these gifts had been accepted, neither Kee-haw or Soon-hee could break the engagement. Even if one died before the wedding, the other must go into mourning for the proper period of time. If Kee-haw had been the one to die, Soon-hee would have been treated like any other widow.

The night before the marriage, the bride-to-be always had her hair done up at the nape of the neck. Before this, Soon-hee had worn a pigtail braided down the middle of her back. Soon-hee's mother and the other older women of the family, who had begun to arrive, helped Soon-hee do her hair. This new knot at the nape was one of the proofs that she had changed her status. She was now an adult. Every hair that was too short to stay in place was pulled out.

This same evening, Wun-sik came around to Kee-haw's to be sure everything was ready. Kee-haw asked him if he had procured the wooden mandarin duck that is used at a wedding. Wun-sik snapped right back, "No! Absolutely not! It's the last thing I would think of doing! Are you completely out of your wits?"

Kee-haw, greatly taken aback, jumped as though shot! "What's the matter? Has something gone wrong?" he asked rather sharply.

"Now don't get excited, friend; you know as well as I that the 'duck' part of the ceremony is to remind everyone and especially the bridal couple of the goose gander, who is faithful to one mate and to one only, all his life. You have decided to break the rule! You don't fit the picture! So forget the duck!"

"Yes, but I will be faithful to my Soon-hee all my life, and I want everyone to know it, so you can just go and get the duck. It's not too late." Kee-haw's eyes glittered with a dangerous fire, and his face turned a swarthier color as he pushed his friend toward the door.

"Now look here, Kee-haw-yah, just stop pushing me. Everything is under good control and you don't have to upset it this late in the day. Have you forgotten the old Chinese proverb, 'One moment of patience may ward off great disaster; one moment of impatience may ruin a whole life'? I know no one likes to be crossed, especially when he's set his heart on something as important as a wedding. But Kee-haw-yah, monogamy has just flown out the window, and a dozen ducks wouldn't change it in the least. So relax and face the facts. Is your lacquer box ready? I've got to take it to Soon-hee-ssee's home, before it gets too late."

"Isn't that funny, Wun-sig-ee, when Sour-face was angry a couple of weeks ago, I was coolness personified. But here and now, a mere wooden duck turned me upside down. Please forgive me, Wun-sik-friend. I'm sorry. Yes, the box is ready, with the skirt and coat for the bride. Will you come back here afterwards, or go on home?"

"Well, it will be quite late by then, and I do want to be here early in the morning, so maybe I should go straight home. That is unless you," and he lowered his voice, "think you'll need me for a bodyguard the rest of the evening." And Wun-sik thumped Kee-haw on the back!

Wun-sik arrived at the Kims' in fifteen or twenty minutes. Ordinarily, the duty is performed by the nearest male relative of the groom. Since none was available, Wun-sik had graciously offered to take his place. However, he had completely forgotten one feature of weddings that Koreans think is amusing. Soon-hee's younger brother had been hiding behind the open gate. As Wun-sik entered the gate-house, this brother rubbed his charcoaled hand all over Wun-sik's right cheek and jaw. Everyone had a big laugh at Wun-sik's expense.

The big, solid rice cake had already been prepared. Soon-hee's father properly installed the lacquer box on top of the big cake and then opened it. After all had admired them, the beautiful skirt and coat were taken to the bride's room.

The first part of the wedding ceremony was always conducted at the bride's home. So about eight the next morning, Kee-haw donned the traditional court dress. He then set out from the home, astride the pony which he had hired with its attendant for the occasion. Kee-haw wore the wide, stiff, embroidered belt. He also wore the traditional hat, decorated in red and green, on the back of his head. The hat had a heavy, silver bar placed horizontally below it. The pony attendant walked briskly at the head of the pony, calling out when necessary to clear the way. Every Korean man is a Prince For A Day, on the day of his wedding, as he proudly wears a prince's garb.

Though the distance across town was short, the important ceremony of riding the pony, (which in Korean is called a horse), was not to be omitted. Soon-hee's family had carefully laid a wide path of rice straw mats all the way across the courtyard, from the Great-Gate entrance to the mah-roo, or front porch. Kee-haw dismounted and doffed his shoes. On one side of the mah-dahng, or courtyard, he saw the table on which the duck is usually placed, with a beautiful screen behind it. Accordingly, part way up to the porch, he paused. Turning ninety degrees, he very deliberately and solemnly bowed the required three half-bows* toward the table.

The neighborhood boys then came forward and guided him the rest of the way to the mah-roo. There he took his place in a sitting position, facing the gate through which he had just come.

As the groom is considered a Prince For a Day, the bride is also considered a Princess. She wears the skirt and coat the groom has sent her the night before. Her garments are many-colored, and the hat she wears is a jeweled coronet. She has a thickly powdered face. Her lips and cheeks are a brilliant red, and her eyes are sealed with honey.

"Come on Soon-hee, it's time for you to make your appearance," her mother coached her. "Don't hesitate, even though you can't see a thing. Just trust your bridesmaids to escort you to the right position in front of the groom. From then on, you know what to do."

When Soon-hee stood before him, Kee-haw was standing again, facing the courtyard gate. If the bride's eyes had been open, they would have been demurely downcast, looking at the floor directly in front of her.

Both of them bowed to each other, Soon-hee twice and Kee-haw once. Due to her sealed eyes, however, Soon-hee's first bow started a bit before Kee-haw's.

Her bows were unique, reserved only for this occasion. She began by putting her right hand on top of her left, both palms down, straight out at the level of her eyes. She then sank down to a position that was first a squat and then a kneel. At the end, she was leaning in the groom's direction, her hands still extended forward.

Kee-haw's was the regular full-bow*. When they had finished their ritual, Kee-haw sat in his former position and Soon-hee sat facing him, a table laden with fruit between them. Kee-haw's legs were crossed, but Soon-hee had one knee up, acknowledging the male superiority.

One bridesmaid then poured some wine into the bowls and handed one to each. Each imbibed some of the wine and passed the remainder to the other. Soon-hee passed the bowl under the table, and Kee-haw, in turn, passed his over the table. They both then sipped wine from the other's bowl. Again she bowed to him twice, and he returned one bow.

All this was done in complete silence.

The officiating woman repeated the process two more times, whereupon Soon-hee arose and retired to her room. Strangely enough, the jujubes* were left untouched but the ceremony itself was now over.

Most of the guests were friends and relatives of the Kims. Many of them had arrived quite early on this wedding day. The few who came from some great distance had arrived the day before.

One person, representing each household of guests, presented an unwrapped gift of money or an item of food to

Soon-hee's parents to help curtail the cost of the wedding. The men presented their gifts to Kim-Miller. The women presented theirs to Soon-hee's mother. Careful record was made of all gifts, for if there was a wedding later at the home of the giver, at least the same amount would be expected in return.

During the wedding day, Soon-hee was neither to smile nor speak a word. If she forgot and allowed herself to smile, she knew that all her children would be girls, the greatest calamity which could befall her, short of being childless. Boys were indispensable because they perpetuated the family name and also conducted the ancestor-worship of departed spirits.

Part of the almost-cruel fun of this day was carried out by children. They did their best to outwit Soon-hee. They tried in every way to catch her off guard and thus force her to smile or speak against her wishes. It was really a game which Soon-hee was determined to win.

As soon as Soon-hee left, Kee-haw rose and went over and bowed once to his father-in-law and once to his mother-in-law. Then the dinner was served to Kee-haw. He ate it alone, right there on the mah-roo, while all the guests watched.

Very thoughtfully, he left quite a bit of each dish, for he knew that as soon as he finished, the rest would be taken to Soon-hee to eat in private.

He finished off a little more rice wine, to the accompaniment of some rather ribald singing on the part of the men.

The Kims had fixed up one of their rooms for the bridal couple. Years ago it had been the men's parlor, or sah-rahng. For quite a few years, though, Kim-Miller had been using it for his office and storeroom. Soon-hee's Mother's ingenuity was sorely taxed to transform this dark, dusty room into a bridal-chamber! She moved most of the stuff onto the side porch where it would be out of the way of the festivities. She sent the younger children out into the hills to gather a nice bouquet of wild iris. She had stacked two of the heavier sacks of grain in one corner of the room and covered them with some attractive leftover trousseau cloth. Several days before the wedding she had built a fire in the appropriate kitchen fireplace, putting some water in the kettle above it, so it wouldn't be damaged. She wanted to be sure that the flues under the awn-dawl were open, and the room would heat properly. Then for a finishing touch, she poured a bit of precious, fresh sesame oil on a clean rag and wiped the entire eight feet square of oil-paper floor with it. When she had finished, the entire room, but especially the floor, shone like new.

The ceremony was over. Everyone had imbibed more rice wine than they could conveniently handle. The bridal couple left, escorted to their room amidst shouting, laughter and more juicy jokes. Soon-hee quickly cleaned her face of the wedding makeup and washed the honey out of her eyes.

Kee-haw shut the door and turned to Soon-hee. "Girl," he started out, "in **my** heart you are no ch'up. I have chosen you because I like you and want you and because you are lovely, good and cheerful. The Paek family has too long been without joy. In the new Paek home there will be a new joy! Maybe I shouldn't say this, but I really hope that you will be happy, too."

Soon-hee knew, as did all Korean women, that the model, dutiful wife was known for her demure, quiet ways. In addition, she knew that the rank of ch'up, or Second-Wife, though fairly common when means permitted, was not an easy one. So she simply remained silent following her husband's remarks.

Kee-haw was quick to notice this and wasted no time in voicing his approval, "Yes, my fondest hopes are realized. You are as modest, sweet and happy as your name implies*. I have listened from afar to the music of your laughter. Now your eyes have been unsealed. You may loosen you lips and speak to me, my bride."

Until now Soon-hee had carefully kept her eyes fixed on the floor, with only one momentary exception. When, out of the corner of her eye, she could see that her husband's feet were turned toward the door, she stole a quick glance at his handsome face.

Now she raised her eyes, and for a brief moment they met his for the first time. Her whole attitude betokened a deep-seated shyness. They were both still standing. A smile spread over Kee-haw's happy face. "You are pretty, my bride, even prettier up close than when I caught stolen glimpses of you through your Great-Gate. I am the luckiest man alive. What more could I ask?"

Very tenderly, he reached out both hands and drew her to him. This was something new and distinctly different. Both felt something they had never felt before. He pulled her pretty head to his shoulder. His cheek felt the fresh coolness of her forehead.

His hand felt the smooth perfection of her lovely, satiny, oriental skin and the gentle curve of her neck. All the short hairs at the base of her hairline had been plucked, while those that were long enough to stay in the bun had been gathered at the nape. The back of his hand brushed the jet-black, glossy bundle.

"I love your shyness, my beauty," he said, "but you do not need to be shy with me. I am your devoted husband. We are not in our own home yet, but this is our wedding night, and no one else is nearby. Always remember that I want your pretty laughter to continue to ring out in our courtyard as long as we live. You are to be my pretty songbird, and your happy laughter will be your song."

At first, Soon-hee pulled back a trifle from his impetuosity, but the caress was enjoyable and very gentle. She soon acquiesced. Suddenly, however, the noise of demanding voices broke into that marvelous moment. They seemed to come from the outer courtyard, but then they drew nearer.

Kee-haw stepped over to the outside door of the small room. It opened onto the inner porch and the rather private back courtyard. He pulled the two-inch ring off the small metal knob, the spike end of which had been driven into the doorpost. He threw the door open.

A man, rather red-faced and out of breath, came around the back corner of the house. "Come quickly, please...both of you," he said between gasps; " the feast...is all ready ...and the food...will be getting cold."

He was properly dressed, with his clothing hitched up to allow freedom for running. He was considerably overweight, and though he had run only the short distance from the village inn, he was puffing like the strange, new steam cars on the shiny, endless rails.

Of course the guests couldn't start until the bridal couple arrived. This gave the occasion for a lot of friendly banter at the expense of the couple. "Such people! Late to their own wedding feast!" Soon-hee, however, remained with the prescribed downcast eyes and did not try to reply to any of the jibes.

Dishes of beef, pork, fowl and dog soaked in honey to represent wealth were arranged on the rather crowded tables. A well-cooked rooster with a red jujube*, or oriental date, in its mouth, was served to make certain that they would never get old. A hen with a peeled, white chestnut, also held in its mouth, insured many sons and grandsons. A heaped-up dish of noodles or vermicelli in seemingly endless strings, symbolized long life. There was also fish, both dried and smoked, as well as at least a dozen varieties of bread, pastry, fruit and candy, besides the inevitable white rice wine.

Except for some queer, rustling noises outside the paper doors, the first night passed uneventfully. As the sun broke through the clouds the next morning, Kee-haw stepped to the door. He was glad that he had arranged for the curtained sedan-chair carried by two men. Kee-haw himself walked over and properly opened it for Soon-hee. Thus was she transported in elegant privacy to her new home. Two bearers were sufficient to carry the articles of dowry.

Kee-haw moved ahead of the procession. Soon-hee's father also had his place as the procession wended its way across the little town. His presence added dignity to the occasion. He would spend the night in the next-door-neighbor's spare room. They entered the Paek courtyard. Kee-haw proudly opened the door of the new, one-room-and-lean-to bridal cottage. The bearers brought the packages and chests to the porch. They slipped out of their shoes and arranged the accoutrements properly inside.

Kee-haw then pulled the curtain of the sedan-chair, or kahmah, and led his wife into their new home. The bearers and the sedan-chair men exchanged knowing looks, grinned silently and withdrew.

Under normal circumstances, a First-Wife would expect to have a sort of three-day honeymoon. During this period, she would have none of the visible obligations of being a housewife. However, Soon-hee understood full well that in her subordinate position of Second-Wife, she could not expect this royal treatment.

Just the same, this was to be their first night together in their own little home. And of course this held an excitement and thrill that was solely theirs. The preceding night at the Kims' had been somewhat formal. Now they were at home, and somehow both Soon-hee and Kee-haw felt that this was really **the** night.

Again they found themselves standing in the middle of the room, in each other's arms. Kee-haw was watching Soon-hee's lips. Surely they would open and say something appropriate to return his love ...Oh! ...they moved a little ...but there was no sound. She was just moistening them with her little tongue. He thrilled. He felt like something very vital and supremely important was stirring inside him! How could something like a tongue be so sweet and precious? Such daintiness! ...and it was all his ... Paek Kee-haw's!

Her lips moved again ..."My Lord, you should be comfortably seated, and I should be waiting on you. This is not seemly." Her words showed her training in the good traditions of Korea, the Hermit Nation. It had an ancient culture of its own and needed no other.

Kee-haw could feel the ecstasy surge through him. Men were not often so lucky in securing a well-bred wife, even in Korea! As he held her close, he wondered if she could feel it, too.

Voice subdued, he said, "Your first words in our new home are eloquent and dutiful. But they are not the words of love that I have waited ten long years to hear, my dove, my songbird. We will have a lifetime in which you may take care of my wants. What I want most now, is to hear from your own mouth that you are still as happy as I have always known you to be."

He sat down on a soft cushion on the floor and pulled another one close. Then he drew her down beside him. "My paw-bae (my jewel), you must be very tired from your preparations for the wedding. There will be no waiting on me tonight! Last night we spent in your parents' home. Tonight we celebrate in **our** home, where no one else has ever lived.

"This is truly our night of love, little one," he said. "Please take down your hair. I've only had glimpses of you as a carefree girl, with your braided hair streaming down your back. Sometimes I saw you through your front gate, or at the village well, or else down by the stream. But all those glimpses were so unsatisfactory, especially if I thought anyone else was looking my way." He paused a moment to reach up and stroke the back of her head.

"But I knew your hair was long and very beautiful and oh ... so jet black." Soon-hee could feel his whole body vibrate at the memory.

Obediently, she pulled out the five inch long, gold hairpin which Kee-haw had sent her. Almost every married woman in ancient Korea wore this type of hairpin at the nape of the neck, though most were silver rather than gold. She leaned back and gave her head a double shake. Out came the heavy folds that the pin had contained, and she began a soft, natural laugh.

But only two or three muted chuckles had come to the surface, when suddenly her shoulders shook and she sobbed convulsively. Tears streamed from her lustrous eyes. She buried her lovely, satiny face in her hands. "I am so fortunate," she sobbed. "You are so good to me ... Do you know, my husband? ... every young Korean girl is deathly afraid of marriage!" Brokenly she spoke. "The old-wives-tales ... of what a man does to her ... fill her with terror ... But you are so kind ... I don't think ... you could ever hurt ... anyone."

Kee-haw helped her off with her outer wedding finery, blew out the little lamp, pulled off his own outer clothes and lay down on the warm floor. This time there was no resistance when he pulled her to him. Her tears were gone. Of her own volition she drew closer. He could feel her shiver slightly with excitement.

As Kee-haw's arms went around her small, supple form, he marveled that human flesh could be so smooth and silk-like in texture. Instinctively he knew his farm hands were too rough for such delicacy. Something deep within him said, "Gently, boy, gently."

And sensing this, she said, "My husband is so strong and so warm. I could lie here forever and be happy." Again those soft, contented chuckles came from her lips, and it sounded to Kee-haw as though they started from way down, 100 lee* below her feet. Only this time there were no sobs.

CHAPTER V
Troubles

Morning crept in very softly and silently in this Land of the Morning Calm. With it the realization came to Kee-haw, would-be master of the enlarged Paek family, that certain relations would have to be ordered and stipulated.

True, First-Wife had done her best to discourage this new affinity before it was firmly established. "But now," he reflected, "she has stayed out of sight, remained quiet and behaved herself during the first night at home. She could have been extremely obnoxious. After all," he pondered, "she does keep the house well, and the children under as fair control as you could expect from a woman."

As soon as he and Soon-hee were dressed, he said, "We must go out now and meet the rest of the family." To his surprise, they were already dressed, hair-combed and breakfast-prepared. Kee-haw tried not to look startled. However, instinctively he suddenly realized that First-Wife was not going to give the ch'up a chance to think that she didn't run a well-ordered household. Being fundamentally honest, Kee-haw had to admit once more that this was true. Of course, First-Wife had somewhat outdone herself this time! A qualm of conscience gave him a slight jolt.

The amenities were attended to without too much awkwardness. But everyone saw how First-Wife looked very austerely, at Soon-hee's face. She seemed to be wondering whether she was still that giggling, carefree thing she'd seen down at the stream-bed laundry-spot, and whether, now that she was married, she would settle down and do her work in better time.

First-Wife gave a slight shrug, as much as to say, "Time will tell, and till then I'll give her the benefit of the doubt." This was fair enough.

Kee-haw's three boys lined up in stair-step order and bowed very solemnly to Soon-hee. They had heared of a ch'up, but this was too sudden and immediate. Soon-hee smiled pleasantly at them. The eldest, Wun-yung, was ten, Korean count*, and the youngest, Wun-bawk, was three. Then his daughter came forward and bowed too. She was five. Soon-hee stepped over and touched her lovely hair. "We are going to be friends," she said, and they both broke into smiles.

Kee-haw sighed inwardly with a sense of relief as he sat down to his meal with his three sons in the inner living/dining/sleeping room. He was very proud of Soon-hee and his children, too. Even First-Wife had behaved as well as could be expected. Soon-hee had very quickly slipped down into the kitchen, right next to the inner room. She tied an old cloth around her for an apron and started cleaning up. She knew her place and was not giving First-Wife a chance to find fault. Kee-haw observed this whenever he glanced down through the half-open door and couldn't suppress a smile.

First-born, Wun-yung, had a school book open beside his little individual table and was studying for an examination as he ate, but he was half-watching his father out of the corner of his eye. This was a memorable morning, and it was quite hard to concentrate. Luckily he caught his dad's smile, and he smiled too. In fact, he almost laughed out loud, for being the eldest, he knew there was fire in the atmosphere, and joy, too. The other boys were busy with their meals and hadn't noticed the smiles.

Wun-yung reached over and touched his father's knee. "I'm glad you're happy, Honorable Father," he whispered very softly, so even the younger brothers wouldn't hear. Kee-haw said nothing, but reached over and patted his son.

After a brief interval he leaned over and encouraged him, "You're studying so hard for you examination, Wun-yung, I know you'll do well. Better get ready. It's almost time to go, and you don't want to be late."

Kee-haw mused over his warm rice-water*. "If only old Sour-face could change her ways. She can do with a little help from a younger woman. It's still a good five or six or even seven years until the first daughter-in-law will come. Of course she'll live with us and wait on her. But this ch'up-arrangement will give her time now to enjoy life a little more and let others enjoy it too." So Kee-haw tried his best to rationalize the situation, justify himself, and pacify his slightly disturbed conscience.

He rinsed his teeth with some of the rice-water and drank the rest. The boys had already finished and excused themselves. The older two picked up their books and paused at the outer door to say good-bye. Both then turned and started running to be sure to get to school on time.

The outside work around the house and in the fields was pretty well caught up. The hard, extra work of building the one-room-and-lean-to-cottage was over. But still there had been no time to relax and rebuild his body and mind. "I'm not going out to the fields today," Kee-haw announced loudly. The paper-door between him and the kitchen had been carefully closed after First-Wife brought in the warm rice-water.

Kee-haw was well aware that both women heard him. Under his breath he muttered, "I'm going to celebrate and feast my eyes on beauty when I can do so unobserved. And incidentally, it won't hurt a bit to see that no quarrels come on this first full day."

He stalked magnificently over to his one-kahn-and-lean-to-house, feeling and looking like a lord in his castle. There he got out an old book of Confucius, put away for just such an occasion as this. He didn't particularly want to read the ancient sage. But somehow this unplanned and unwonted leisure seemed to heighten his "Lordly Feeling" and he surmised that a true Lord would spend much time studying or at least reading Kawng-jah*, (Confucious).

He sat over near the door where he could glance out at intervals through the two-inch square of glass. He had been very fortunate to locate and buy it in the big city and had carefully installed it in the paper-door. The pane was just at the right height to look out, as one sat on the floor. Since the room was comparatively dark inside most of the time, no one could tell when he chose to look out. And if he sat close to the door with the light streaming through the pane, reading would be much easier.

Several times during the morning he had brief but rewarding glimpses of his new bride. She strove to outdo Wun-yung's Honorable Mother in keeping busy with all sorts of jobs. She was evidently trying to foresee any jobs that entailed lifting in order to spare the older woman. Kee-haw congratulated himself that she was older than the other girls in town. In fact, she was not too very much younger than First-Wife. This should make it harder for Wun-yung's Mother to make life too miserable for her. At least this is what he wistfully hoped.

Kee-haw had trouble keeping his mind on his rather dry reading. After all, he could read Confucius anytime! Confucius had managed somehow to last a few years already and would probably last for a few more! Repeatedly he found his lovely, old, cord-bound book lying idly on his knees. His thoughts were ten thousand lee from Confucius and his sage sayings. Several times during the latter hours of the morning, he heard a voice raised in irritable tones. He sensed that all was not gold, even if some of it glittered.

Half-guiltily, he recalled that First-Wife was really quite efficient and capable. Was his taking of a second-wife expecting too much of her? Had he let his desire for what he thought was understanding, joy and love lead First-Wife and him into an impossible triangle? Of course, as Wun-sik had affirmed, dual marriage was as old as the mountains. But maybe heartache and frustration were too! Maybe he should think of ways to restore her loss of face. Possibly she had also lost a certain sense of security that having to share her man with another woman might entail!

These were deeper and more complicated thoughts than he had ever had before. Even the great sage Confucius didn't seem to have any particular light to throw on this subject.

"Maybe I should read this book more attentively with this problem in mind," he concluded.

And then, as an afterthought, he added, "The Great God of Heaven must be far greater than Confucius or any other wise man! Maybe He has discovered some way of enlightening us poor mortals as to what is good and what is bad, what is better and what is worse."

But how about Soon-hee, the sweet woman he had chosen himself? He loved her more already than he could love Sourface in a hundred years. What did this mean to her? Had he only brought sorrow and grief to a happy heart? True, he had been listening to his own heart and the tongue of his best friend, Wun-sig-ee.

Even the youngest child who has attended a School of the Chinese Classics for a few months knows the ancient Chinese ideogram for "peace*." It depicts only one woman under one roof! "Well, we'll see," he thought. "Things will naturally be difficult on this first day."

But at least he resolved that he would not shut his eyes and think only of himself and his own needs and joys. First-Wife had hurt him too much for him to be the willing instrument for bringing hurt to anyone else. Least of all would he hurt his precious Darling. On that never-to-be forgotten yester-eve, had she not read his heart and known this very thing? She was more than just another woman. They had looked into each other's hearts, and looking, loved.

Kee-haw wandered over to the old living-room. First-Wife brought in the lunch on a small individual table. She did the subsequent waiting on him. Lunch was decidedly boring. Wun-yung's Honorable Mother was meticulous about closing the door each time she entered and left. He couldn't change his position or crane his neck. She managed it very cleverly. Never once did he catch a single glimpse of his sweetheart, though she was so near. Here he had really hoped to see her at closer range than across the courtyard!

He felt somewhat better when he got back into the new cottage. She must have left some of her fragrance there. From his place by the tiny window, he could look right into the kitchen, though it was too dark to see much of anything. In fact, this was the very reason the outside kitchen door was usually left open.

Somehow, this dear cottage seemed to be just the place in which to indulge in some more daydreaming! In Kee-haw's mind, Confucius had completely lost even the knee position and was now relegated to the floor beside him. Was there something the matter with him? Was he, whom everyone knew as a hard-working farmer, a he-man, or wasn't he?

His somewhat depressing reverie had only been resumed a few minutes, when it was suddenly broken by a piercing scream. Hair disheveled and streaming behind her, Soon-hee was racing across the courtyard toward the cottage!

Back of her, not making quite as good speed, came Wun-yung's Mother, brandishing the charcoal-shovel! She was shrieking, "They're the Master's own words. He said that you were going to help me by doing the heavy housework. I'm only following his orders, so there!"

Kee-haw got the door open in time for Soon-hee to rush in, without removing her shoes, an unheard of trespass! She'd naturally had them on, working on the dirt floor of the kitchen.

"Save me," she screamed, "she's trying to kill me!" Wun-yung's Honorable Mother stopped at the stoop.

"All I did was ask her to fill our two big water-jars from the village well. She's no weakling! Why did she stop when she was only half through?" Tears were streaming down Soon-hee's face and spotting her new pink jacket. She had evidently thought her life was in danger.

Kee-haw heaved a big, audible sigh, "You women will be the end of me yet! This is an easy one, Wun-yung's Honorable Mother. It takes four or five trips with the small jar to fill one of the big ones, right? Today is the first-day-after, and all the young girls at the well are jealous of Soon-hee's good luck! There are just too many jokesters among them.

"If you don't want to finish the water-carrying job yourself, we can get along for half a day with a half-supply, and if Soon-hee goes again very early tomorrow morning, she won't be tormented to death. Now both of you run along! Can't you see I'm busy reading? And both of you behave yourselves. I don't want any more of this foolishness! If there's trouble, bring it to me. It's too difficult for you to try to settle it yourselves."

Speaking of troubles, during the following winter poor Wun-sik had more than his share: Acute double pneumona visited his wife. None of the herb-teas seemed to help and the moo-nyu's* incantation and incense burnings only seemed to make his wife worse. In less than two weeks she was gone. After the funeral, Kee-haw visited his friend for several hours every day for a week. During the following week, he spent several hours with him daily in his fields, helping him catch up his lost time.

CHAPTER VI
The Missionary

By now it was about mid-afternoon. The two older boys came back from the School of the Chinese Classics, commonly called the Room of Writing*. Suddenly a loud cough was heard at the tae-moon, the Great-Gate of the courtyard. Second-Son ran out to the gate. (He was always more alert than Wun-yung.) Kee-haw glanced inquisitively in that direction through the tiny window. After a slight pause, Tool-jjae came running straight toward him.

Kee-haw pushed open the door. The lad stopped on the stone-step in front of the porch. "Honorable Father, there is an Honorable Guest at the gate."

"Well, why didn't you invite him in?" Kee-haw queried, half-rebukingly.

The boy had slipped out of his shoes and stepped up on the porch. He lowered his voice and leaned close to his father, "But I've never seen him before! How did I know it was safe to ask him in, Father? And anyway, his skin is a funny white color." He dropped his voice some more and whispered, "Maybe he has leprosy! Really, father, you'd better go see!"

"Good observation, son." Slipping into his shoes, Kee-haw went quickly to the gate, appearing to be taking the deliberate strides of a gentleman.

He took one glance. This was no ordinary man. This man stood quite tall and erect, more like the northern Koreans. But judging by his clothes, he was probably from some other part of the world, or even from some other world! At least his clothing was rather neat and somewhat becoming. It occurred to Kee-haw that he might be a man of some standing among his own people. Certainly he was not from any of the neighboring villages where Kee-haw had been.

Without further delay, Kee-haw bowed very low, "Welcome to my humble abode, Honorable Guest." He bowed a second time and courteously waved this pale-skinned stranger toward the new cottage. With a little excusable pride he thought, "It's such a nice clean place in which to receive special guests." As they walked across the courtyard together, Kee-haw wondered what could possibly have brought a complete stranger to his home. He couldn't remember such a thing ever happening before, unless a peddler had come, bringing his wares with him. No wonder his young son had been wary!

Truly, it was almost as if he were entertaining a visitor from another world! But was such a thing possible? How would they converse? Did this gentleman speak Korean, or was there some sort of sign-language they could use that would satisfactorily take its place? True, he had spoken to the guest in Korean, but he had also waved him in the right direction to the new house!

Opening the door, Kee-haw again bowed from his hips, very low. The gentleman thanked him in Korean and removed his strange-looking, black shoes. He then stepped over the threshold, ducking his head very naturally as he entered the low door.

Kee-haw hadn't even noticed it earlier in the day, but now he looked quickly around and mentally registered deep gratitude to Soon-hee. She had carefully covered her clothes that hung on the wall. She had also folded the new bedding of the previous night, putting it in the high wall-closet and shutting the door.

This quick inventory of the room took a second or two while the guest was seating himself in the honored place which Kee-haw indicated. Kee-haw apologized, "I'm sorry the room is cold. It's so early, we've just started the fire for tonight. If you will be so kind as to prolong your visit awhile, the floor will be more comfortable. And now, let us greet each other." He lowered his body to the floor, but his legs were under him in what was practically a kneeling position. He put both hands in front of him, palms down on the floor and bowed low, "As for my name, it is Paek Kee-haw."

The stranger returned the salutation very properly in like manner with "This person is Ahn Euee-wah. This is the first time I've had the pleasure of seeing your Honorable Self, Paek Teacher. Are you in peace?"

"Yes, are you in peace?" Kee-haw returned. They both came back to the sitting position. Then they crossed their legs in what looked to be a very uncomfortable posture, with the right feet bottom up, on top of the left knees. They sat this way for a few minutes. Then, Kee-haw spoke again, "Please sit comfortably." He suited the action to the words and recrossed his legs so both feet were on the floor.

As the host, Kee-haw again took the initiative, "You are not from this immediate vicinity. Where is your honorable dwelling place, Honorable Guest?"

"You are absolutely correct, Honorable Lord-man," Mr. Ahn replied. "I'm a westerner from Mee-gook*, the Beautiful Country east of here, across the Great Peaceful Ocean. I live in Maw-see-paht now, the county seat. There's a Jesus Church there. I understand that you are one of the outstanding men of Moo-jee-moo. As there are no Jesus-Believers in your village, I thought I would visit you, Paek Teacher. You are very kind to invite me in, a stranger, when I'm sure you must be busy.

"I would like to offer a present to you and your family. This is a copy of one of the four Good News books, which are really biographies of Jesus. If you will read this, you will learn how the Great God of Heaven wants you to be exceedingly happy," Ahn finished.

Kee-haw could hardly wait for a chance to reply. "My goodness, Ahn Teacher, those are the very things I was pondering this morning. But . . . not so fast please! Yes, Maw-see-paht I know and have visited many times on market days. I suppose the Jesus Church is the rather large building that everyone calls 'the Meeting-Place.' But who in the world is Jesus, and who are the Jesus-Believers you mentioned a moment ago?" Kee-haw leaned over and pushed the door open. "Excuse me," he said to Ahn.

"Wun-yung's Mother," he called. "Send the boys over to meet the guest. And first, quickly send Wun-yung. I have an errand for him."

Turning back to Ahn, he continued, "You are very kind to give such a nice present to someone you have never seen before. But please answer my questions."

"You are right about the Meeting-Place. Yes, that's the building all right. Now let me introduce you to Jesus. He is the Great God of Heaven, Hah-nah-nim's only . . ." Just then, Wun-yung came running to the door. He had stepped out of his shoes before he crossed the clean wooden porch to his father, who was still holding the door open.

Kee-haw leaned toward him and whispered, "Son, in a moment I want all three of you to meet our guest. But first tell the women to take some dried persimmons and make us a drink. Now hurry!"

Instead of running back, Wun-yung stepped in over the threshold and closed the door behind him. He cupped his hand to his father's ear and whispered something back. But he could have saved the effort, for at that precise moment, without warning, the door popped open.

First-Wife stood there with a wooden tray in her hand. There were five bowls on the tray. Four were celadon porcelain, gray-green, olive shade, reminiscent of a culture thousands of years old. There was also a smaller one that was a creamy-white. The woman had put on a clean white jacket, beautifully ironed, and a white apron, and had tidied her hair.

She came in, kneeled, put the tray on the floor and bowed low to the guest. Kee-haw volunteered, "This is the Inside Person."

Ahn acknowledged with a bow, "Yes, are you in peace?"

The handleless cups were filled with a beautiful amber-colored liquid. Pine-nuts floated on top. Kee-haw couldn't help wondering which one of the wives had been so alert to the situation. First-Wife handed the first cup to the guest. In stocking feet, the other two boys joined their brother, slipping noiselessly into the room.

Ahn looked up and saw them lined up in front of him. They were on their knees and in proper stair-step order, waiting for him to receive their greeting. They wore their best clothes. Outstanding was Wun-bawg-ee, the three-year-old, with his gorgeous sleeves of many colors. Ahn was reminded of Joseph's coat. It was a solemn moment, but also very touching, as each lad tried to look serious and give his greeting properly.

Ahn Pastor had difficulty holding back a smile of approval. Each boy placed both his hands in front of him, pigeon-fingered, palms flat on the floor and bowed until his forehead touched the floor. Ahn gravely returned the bows and listened attentively as their father recited their names. Then his face relaxed and he ventured a slight smile, as he complimented, "Such polite and dignified young gentlemen! God has been good to you both. Tell me, have you no daughters?"

In the meantime, First-Wife had served Kee-haw and the boys their hot drinks. Wun-bawg-ee in his colorful jacket was very pleased with his little white cup, different from all the others. He kept looking sideways at his older brothers to be sure he both held the cup and drank properly. He had difficulty getting his little chubby fingers to hold it just right. The drink was delicious and he smacked his lips with sheer delight, as did also the older ones! How else could those who had prepared the drinks know how much the recipients appreciated their efforts?

"Oh yes, Ahn-Teacher," Kee-haw replied, "but we luckily have only one daughter, and of what use are girls anyway? Sure, they help around the house, but they're such a needless expense. And after a very few years, the wedding can be almost as burdensome as a funeral. I know perfectly well that a big wedding gives your family prestige, but is it worth it?" Kee-haw paused and called toward the closed paper door, "Third, come here."

By the time First-Wife had backed out the door, crossed the porch and got into the right pair of shoes, a bright face appeared around Mom's voluminous skirt. Third shyly sidled around to her father, stealing glances at the guest. She went through the same routine as her brothers. Since she was "only a girl," no one had thought to provide her a cup of persimmon drink. She'd probably sampled it with the two women out in the kitchen anyway. Nevertheless, she sat a bit disconsolate behind the boys.

Ahn addressed Kee-haw, "My friend, you asked me some important questions awhile ago, and I'm afraid I only partially answered them. Please forgive me. You were asking who Jesus is and who Believers are. Very simply put, Jesus is the Great God of Heaven, Hah-nah-nim's only Son. He loved us so very much, He came to earth to live among us and to show us God's true way of life. He died for us so that we could live the God-Way, which is the Way of Peace and Joy. Those who believe this and practice it are the ones who are called Christians or Jesus-Believers.

"Some day, when the Big Market falls on Sunday, bring Wun-yung's Honorable Mother and the family to Maw-see-paht. Drop in to the two o'clock Worship Meeting. You'll be most welcome. And in the meantime you can prepare yourselves for this by reading the small Good News book."

Ahn stood up to go. "Paek Teacher," he said, "you and your wife have a delightful family. I am indeed fortunate that you were home and I could meet you all . . . . that is, . . I presume . . this is all."

Kee-haw had been smiling expansively, rather proud of his progeny. But this last remark caught him off-guard. On any other day, he would have quickly excused himself out of the awkward moment. But all day his mind and emotions had been filled with lovely thoughts of his newest acquisition! Before he knew it, he was stuttering, "Well . . . that is . . . I mean . . . yes, no . .. there is . . a-n-n-nother."

"Oh, excuse me," said Ahn Pastor and resumed his seat. "Of course, I would very much like to meet them all. You mean a parent is still living?"

"No . . . that is . . . no . . . neither of them is living. There is . . . another . . . . w-w-wife. W-w-we were married yesterday."

"Congratulations," Ahn replied. "Oh, . . now I see. This is her new home. How thoughtful of you! Paek-Teacher, please don't take me wrong, but you must be quite well-to-do!"

Kee-haw gently told the children that they had fulfilled the rules of honoring guests. He said, "Run along children! Change your clothes and go out and play."

Wun-yung, the oldest, went out last. Kee-haw detained him, saying in a muted voice, "Tell her to come here."

While they waited for Soon-hee, Kee-haw continued, "Wun-yung's Honorable Mother is quite impossible! Today she was on her good behavior. Most of the time she is a terror, shrieking at the children, quarreling with the neighbors and complaining about everything, including me! For the last five years of our ten years of marriage, in fact from the time she presented me with that female child, there has been no peace under our roof. Sir, I tell you, a man can't live like that."

The door opened, and winter changed to spring for both men as Soon-hee stepped over the sill. She quickly dropped to her knees, and gave two low oriental curtsies, one to her husband and then one to Ahn.

"Ahn Teacher, this is Kim Soon-hee. I don't know quite why I am telling you so much, a man from another part of the world," Kee-haw went on, "except you have a caring face and are concerned. You know, if it weren't for your Korean name, Ahn Teacher, I could imagine that you really were from another world! Anyway, as long as I have told you some of what is past, let me add this; Soon-hee and I love each other very much. She already understands my heart, and in ten years, Wun-yung's Mother out there, never has."

"Paek teacher, I'm pleased to meet all your family. I do care that you and your first wife have been unhappy." As the missionary turned to go, he said "I'll come to visit again when I'm in your village. However, you will probably be in Maw-see-paht much oftener. Please come up to my house at the west end of town on East Mountain. I'll be more than glad to talk things over and do anything that I can to help. Please think of me as your friend, or if it helps any," and Ahn gave a warm smile, "your friend from another world!"

With the evening meal finished half an hour ago, the busy noises from the kitchen were gradually diminishing. The older boys were busy with their lessons, reading them aloud in old-school fashion. Third's eyelids drooped, and little Wun-bawk had already fallen asleep.

Kee-haw rose and gave a big audible yawn. He stepped over and opened the kitchen door. Addressing Soon-hee he said, "I'm going over to your room and read awhile, where it's more quiet. You might put more fuel on the fire. It feels cooler this evening and the floor wasn't too warm when I came over to supper awhile ago." He sauntered over, lit the small kerosene lamp and sat in the clean-smelling room, thinking, "A veritable Paw-bae, jewel! That's what she is and that will be my name for her, at least when we are alone."

In no time, Soon-hee's muffled cough let him know she was at the door, asking to come in. Quickly he said, "Paw-bae-yah, come in and don't bother to announce yourself to me again. This is your room, your home. And Paw-bae-yah, you've just come from your own private kitchen in the lean-to and from stoking the fire for this room. Any time Sour-face gets too sour, come here and cook a meal for us two. We'll eat by ourselves, in our own palace, my little Queen."

Again he placed both his arms under her short jacket against the naked skin of her solid, silken waist. He pulled her up close to let Soon-hee know she was being hugged from head to toe. And in every spot that he touched her, he felt sparks of live fire race through him.

He pulled himself away, held her at arm's length, and said, "They tell me that they have electricity in our capital city of Seoul. Let's send word to the newspaper that the new Queen of Moo-jee-moo has brought it to her new palace." Both their laughs were soft, radiant and selfless.

He caught one hand and pulled her over near the one-candle-power lamp. "Paw-bae-yah, would you like me to read you an old Korean love story? Sit down here very close to me. Now, your Honor, my Queen," and he pulled out his well-worn book, "you and I will begin to live as life was meant to be lived."

CHAPTER VII

New Concepts

Some days later, as Kee-haw was weeding his winter wheat he recalled something Ahn had said. Ahn had inadvertently let the words drop the day he came. He had said that "Jesus came to earth to show us God's true way of life." He had also said that "this same Jesus died so we could live this true God-Way, which is the Way of Peace and Joy." These were the only words he had ever heard that gave any hope for peace under his roof. And the war between the wives had not diminished as he had hoped. "I must look into this," he thought. "Of course the idea of there being an Honorable God of the Heavens, Hah-nah-nim, is not new, but this idea that He is concerned about every individual's hurts and unhappiness and wants to help and heal is certainly new and confusing. How does anyone know so much about God's feelings? Maybe I'll find out if I go to one of their meetings!"

The next Sunday was not a market day in the county-seat, but Kee-haw decided to go anyway. By rising earlier than usual, he could get almost a day's work done by noon. He could leave around twelve-thirty and still get to the meeting on time. **After** all, it was only fifteen lee to Maw-see-paht. He'd ask Soon-hee to fix him a lunch he could eat while he walked.

With his mind open to the new idea that the God of Heaven, Hah-nah-nim, wanted to give him and his family Peace and Joy and that it was up to him to go after it, the rest of the week went by with a fair amount of equilibrium. Before he knew it, Sunday arrived and Kee-haw left as planned. With nothing to delay him, he found himself welcomed and seated on the floor of the Meeting-Place, at a few minutes before two.

Kee-haw had never seen a room as large as this. A curtain, higher than a man's head, stretched right down the middle of the room, clear to the back. Only men and boys were on his side of the curtain. A man soon came over to greet him. He carried two books, a big and a little one, and sat down beside him. He explained to Kee-haw that the big book was the Word of God, and the little book contained the words of the songs they sang. He laid both of them on the floor in front of them.

The two men bowed to each other and exchanged names and salutations. Someone at the end of the room, talking quite loudly, called out a number in the Chahn-sawng-gah, or hymnbook. Everyone snatched up their smaller books and found the page with the called-out-number. Then a fierce-looking man, with an alarming mustache, and a vicious looking stick, resembling a scaled down billy-club, in his hand, stood up. Kee-haw wondered if all the men on his side of the dividing curtain were going to put up with this husky. Would they let him go ahead and do whatever he was bent on doing?

But no one seemed particularly concerned. Kee-haw remained tense, however, to avoid being caught off guard. Just then he caught sight of Ahn, up near the front. Kee-haw stood up to greet him, but his new volunteer-friend quickly grabbed his too-roo-mah-gee* and pulled him back down. "Worship has started," he whispered. At that moment, everyone, including the hundred women on the other side of the curtain, opened their mouths simultaneously and started wailing. It was quite remarkable!

Kee-haw wondered if, possibly, this new friend who was coaching him was the person the man with the club was getting ready to cudgel. But, no, he just stood there warming up by waving it back and forth. Kee-haw thought, "I guess I'm as brave as the rest of them when it comes to personal danger, if there really is any, but I don't like to see somebody else get hurt unnecessarily."

The man next to him, with the small book open, held it over in front of Kee-haw. The words on the page he pointed to were written in separate groups of four or five lines each.

74

The wailing seemed to be about the same for each group. The fierce man was still warming up. Kee-haw wondered why he kept it up for so long. And where was the poor guy he was after? Or, perhaps, this fierce fellow's waving of the stick was connected to the wailing? He tried to ask his new friend next to him, but he wouldn't stop wailing long enough to answer.

After the last group of words on the page in the Chahn-sawng-gah, they stopped, as did the warming-up of the husky. "My!" thought Kee-haw, "I guess I can relax now. The danger must be over. But somebody should explain to newcomers the purpose of the warming-up and wailing, and what to do next."

Again he stood up to go and see his friend, Ahn. This time, his new friend with the books was looking the other way. He had gotten better than half way there, when he felt a rather rough jerk on his arm from behind. That same 'new friend' had followed and grabbed him. His lower jaw protruded as he said, "Worship is not finished. You're disturbing everyone. Come back!"

Kee-haw thought, "I've been sitting there seven or eight minutes. How long do they expect me to sit still and do nothing? Whoever heard of not greeting your friend when you see him?" There were too many new ways of doing things, and Paek wasn't sure that he was going to like this Jesus Church or these Jesus-Believers.

During this time, Ahn just sat there. He didn't seem to be doing anything in the meeting. Wasn't he important? Wasn't he a leader? Why didn't somebody answer these questions? Now they bowed their heads and shut their eyes! Maybe that was why they didn't answer. Or was it because he hadn't asked?

Kee-haw decided to try again, "Look here, friend, why doesn't Ahn Teacher come over and greet me? He said he was my friend from another world."

The 'new friend' kept his eyes tightly closed and held his finger to his lips as you do to a noisy child. Someone at the other end of the room stopped talking. Then, as if by magic, everybody gave a signal, "Ah-men," at the same time, and everyone's eyes popped open.

"I wonder how long it took them to learn how to do those things simultaneously? Christians seem to be pretty smart people, except that no one seemed to be afraid when that fierce fellow waved his stick. Now everyone seems to be picking up that other book and looking for some special place. And another man up in front is reading loudly from a similar one. Now, once more everyone wails, only this time they all stand up and wail. I guess that's alright. I'm sure tired from sitting so long," Kee-haw mused.

Now another man, with an even louder voice, started to talk. Everyone looked at him and listened intently. Some were even shaking their heads up and down. "Maybe I should listen, too! Then I'd know if I agreed with these head-shakers," Kee-haw thought.

This louder-voiced fellow didn't seem to be talking to any one person. He'd look at a spot on the ceiling for awhile and talk to it. Then he'd look at one individual for a few seconds. Then he'd look at the kerosene lamp, hanging from the ceiling, or at someone on the women's side of the curtain, and so it went.

To Kee-haw, this latter act seemed unfair and breaching some code. No other man was allowed to look so boldly at the women, since the curtain was too high, even when everyone stood to wail. However, Kee-haw decided that since this was his first time at the Meeting-Spot, he would not call him on the breach!

Again Kee-haw came back to his former inspiration, "Maybe I should listen, too!" If Hah-nah-nim was going to bring him the Joy and Peace as Ahn had said he would, he would have to pay attention and find out how. This first time there were so many mysteries! The waving, wailing and reading certainly hadn't brought any Joy and Peace. Maybe listening was the way to get it! Well then! By all the goblins and devils and evil spirits in the world, he would listen, even if it was the last thing he did!

Why in the world did one hundred and fifty or more people have to put up with all this waving and wailing if only listening to the talking was the way to get Peace and Joy? Maybe they were preparing, getting ready, so their minds could receive the Peace and Joy. Well, he'd ask Ahn afterward, but right now he'd better listen!

Kee-haw stretched his cramped legs. He settled down to listen. With his mental meanderings, he had lost the first half of the talking part!

Later on in the meeting, as Kee-haw's critical attitude mellowed, he felt he was slowly beginning to understand. He also felt that the words he was hearing might contain important, if not tremendous, possibilities. He even felt a tingle of anticipation as he thought of them.

The speaker was talking about "The Second Most Important Command." He quoted Jesus as saying that this command was to love each other. He also said, "Of course, you must love God with all your heart first, which is the **most** important command. If you don't obey this first command, you won't obey the second."

Kee-haw thought, "This is good talk, I know, but what does it have to do with acquiring Joy and Peace? That's really why I came and what I need. Why can't we just skip these other things. Why should I love Sour-face, anyway? She likes to be unhappy and unloved. She enjoys thinking everyone is against her! On the other hand, if I'd quit asking myself these questions, I might hear the answers that the speaker gives us." So Kee-haw listened more carefully.

"Some beautiful flowers have thorns. Beauty and sweet smells often come with pain. God has never promised freedom from problems, from decision making, from mistakes or even from pain and hurt. But He does promise that when you are reviled and persecuted and lied about **because** you are His followers, you can be happy! In fact, be **very glad**!"

"Ah! There it is," thought Kee-haw, "and on my first trip to the Meeting Place! Happiness is possible even in the midst of suffering and the speaker's subject isn't even 'Peace and Joy!' "

The speaker continued: "Love God, love each other, the two primaries of a good life. Do these and it doesn't matter what hurts you suffer as His followers, you will still have exceeding Joy and Peace." Kee-haw thought, "What a marvelous idea. It must have come straight from God. Certainly I would never have thought it possible."

Everybody wailed through another numbered page of the Chahn-sawng-gah. Then they bowed their heads for a short time while someone said something about God, Jesus, and a Spirit. That strange signal came again. Everyone started for the doors. That is, everyone except his new friend.

He laid his hand on Kee-haw's arm and in a very pleasant friendly voice said, "Now we will go to see the Ahn-Pastor. I'm awfully sorry; it was entirely my fault! I should have explained to you at the beginning. Worship begins when the first hymn in the Chahn-sawng-gah starts. We stay wherever we are until the close of the last prayer or benediction. It sends us out for the week with God's blessings of Peace and Joy.

"But here's Ahn-Mawk-sah. Are you in peace, Ahn-Mawk-sah? Paek-Teacher, here, says that he knows you and, in fact, that you are a very special friend. I had trouble keeping him from going forward to greet you during the middle of the service!"

Ahn smiled a very pleasant smile and took Paek's right hand in both of his. "Certainly you wanted to come. How should you know it wasn't the right time? Honorable Chun-Elder, of course you explained?"

"Oh yes, and I apologized for not explaining earlier," Chun replied.

"Now, Paek-Teacher, please bring Chun-Elder with you and come with me to meet the Pastor. Almost everyone has left by now, so we should be able to have a leisurely chat with him. You'll find he's a warm-hearted and understanding person. Before we get there, let me tell you that his surname is Lee. I believe you have some Lees in Moo-jee-moo, don't you?"

By then, they had reached the main door. Lee Mawk-sah was saying goodbye to the last few church-folks. "Ahn Mawk-sah, are you in peace?" he greeted the American. "I see you have a newcomer with you. Where are you from, Honorable Guest?"

"You beat me to it, Lee Mawk-sah," Ahn interrupted. "This is the gentleman, Paek Kee-haw-ssee, from Moo-jee-moo, who is looking for peace under his roof. He has come a long way from Moo-jee-moo in the heat of the day, to hear you exposit the words of life. Please greet each other."

"Yes, of course, Paek Teacher. I trust that Chun Elder has already made you feel at home. He certainly has a knack for spotting honorable guests, and easing them over the initial rough spots. We are greatly honored that you came this far to attend our Worship Service, or rather God's Worship Service. But I am tardy in introducing myself. They call this inferior person, Lee Wun-yung*. Are you in peace?"

"No, I'll be frank with you, Lee Mawk-sah, I am not in peace. That is why I left my work on the farm and came to hear you. I want to find peace. I can see that it is going to take many such Sundays and much reading of the Good News books to understand God's Way of Peace and Joy, but I want to especially thank you for the last few words of your talk this morning.

"You spoke straight to my heart, even though your subject was not Peace and Joy. Is it possible for Hah-nah-nim to sometimes speak through humans, when He sees that his children are hurt?"

"Isn't that wonderful"? Lee rejoined. "I saw you sitting with Chun Elder this morning, but I had no idea who you were. Hah-nah-nim must have put those closing words into my mouth. God bless you, Paek Teacher, and, in His own time, may He give you what you crave; but please remember, Hah-nah-nim has never promised to eliminate the thorns. If we want roses, we must accept the thorns, too! But why do we stand here? It's still early. Why don't we all go over to the sah-rahng? We might as well sit while we talk."

Lee Pastor suited the deed to the word and started to walk over to his study. He had already taken one of Kee-haw's hands and at first was pulling him along, too. Only Chun Elder, started off the opposite way, saying, "My wife's calling me, but I'll see you later."

In a few moments, Mrs. Lee had placed a cup of pale barley tea before each of the men and retired into the kitchen. They sat together, relaxed and comfortable. Kee-haw was so enthusiastic over his discoveries of the last hour that he couldn't wait for his host to open the conversation, "I'm sorry, but I don't quite understand. I take it that both of you are ministers; at least I hear them calling both of you, 'Mawk-sah.' But why does Ahn Mawk-sah invite me to come to your Jesus Church, Lee Mawk-sah? Excuse me for being so dense, but as you already know, I'm just a farmer."

"It's true, Paek friend, that I usually preach at this church on Sundays. Once in awhile, I ask Ahn Mawk-sah to occupy the pulpit, which is our way of saying 'conduct the service and preach the sermon.' But that doesn't make this church my church, Paek friend. Every church is God's Church or Jesus's Church, as you have correctly said. Hah-nah-nim and the people of this church have called me to be their servant, in this church and this community. I trust you understand that it's a great honor to be the servant of the Great God of Heaven and his people. Does this answer your question, Paek friend?"

At this point, Ahn said, "I should have explained some of these things to you earlier, Paek Teacher, though maybe they are not really so important. I have under my care a few small country-churches that as yet cannot support a minister. In other words, I am their servant. I was serving Hah-nah-nim here before there were any Korean pastors. In fact, I began here when there were few if any Korean Protestant Christians. So I serve as a big brother to all of them in North Kyung-sahng Province."

Kee-haw answered, "I guess that wasn't such an important thing. I only want to get things straight from the beginning. But please tell me why the man with the stick and the fierce mustache was warming up every so often."

"Sorry, Kee-haw-ssee, that stick is what the song-leader uses to mark the time so that everyone sings together," Ahn further explained.

An hour later, Kee-haw excused himself as he rose, "I'm sorry, but we country-folk have to take care of our livestock. And, oh yes, Lee Pastor, what Chinese characters are the ones you use in your given name? You know, it's just possible that they're the same as those of my First-born Rascal*. The pronunciation is the same all right."

With his right forefinger, Lee Pastor traced the characters of his given name Wun-yung on the palm of his left hand. "Sure enough, they're exactly the same. That makes me very happy, Lee Mawk-sah. Please have a good week. Remain in peace yourself and bring peace to many. And Ahn Mawk-sah, don't forget your promise to come back to Moo-jee-moo before too long. You know, with a name like yours*, just being around you helps." With a slight wave of one hand, Kee-haw crossed the courtyard to the Great-Gate.

"Go in peace," both Lee and Ahn called after him. Then turning to Lee, Ahn said, "You know, when Kee-haw becomes a sincere Christian, he'll get his family affairs straightened out. And his example to all of Moo-jee-moo should help a church grow rapidly there. God is good."

CHAPTER VIII

New Converts And New Troubles

Ahn, as he had promised, revisited Moo-jee-moo on a Wednesday night, two and a half weeks later. He had already finished his fall itineration of the "few small country churches" he'd mentioned to Kee-haw. The Presbytery had appointed him Moderator of their Sessions. Several of them were so small and weak that no congregant had yet progressed to the status of "full communicant member." Two or three had male deacons, but no elders. This meant that only a few of the 35 churches had organized, active Sessions.

Most of Kee-haw's fields faced the same side of Moo-jee-moo as the road to Maw-see-paht. So, like the father of the prodigal son, Kee-haw saw Ahn approaching while he was still a great way off. He dropped his tool where it was and ran to meet him. "Oh, Ahn-Mawk-sah, I was just thinking about you and wondering when you would keep your promise to come back. Then you appeared, like an angel from High Heaven! Excuse me! I'm so excited! Are you in peace?"

"Of course, Paek-friend, but how about you and your nice family? You know, I think a lot of you, and I'm praying and hoping that you will come regularly to the Bible Class and Church. And there's a Communicants' Class that's starting soon. I've also been praying that you will mature in The Faith very quickly. I believe God has given you leadership qualities for the new church in Moo-jee-moo.

"Now, I know I've come early today, Kee-haw-ssee. I don't want you to lose time from your work; but I want to chat with First-Wife before the boys get home from school. I'll go on into town while you work awhile. Fair enough?"

"That sounds marvelous," Kee-haw answered. "If I knew more about prayer and praying I would be praying for you and Wun-yung's Mother while I work, Ahn-Mawk-sah. All I can say is, 'God be with you and bless you.' Go in peace."

Ahn proceeded into town and soon found himself at the Great-Gate of the Paek home. He gave the customary cough, and realizing that it was Soon-hee who had come to open it, he had his fingers to his lips before she had gotten the heavy door open. "I want to see First-Wife for a little while, before the boys get back. I see you have Fourth on your back," he said in a very subdued voice. "Ask Third to stay with you, and see if you can get First-Wife to let you take over whatever she is doing, please." Then, in normal tones, "It's been a long time since I've seen you. Are you dwelling in peace?"

Soon-hee returned the salutation and led him to the sah-rahng, so First-Wife wouldn't feel she had to straighten up the Family Room and thus waste some of his time.

Soon First-Wife, wiping her hands on her apron, came in and bowed. Salutations were exchanged. Ahn explained that he didn't want Kee-haw to lose time from his farming, so he had come ahead. He added that he only hoped he wasn't interrupting any important work. Her eyes lit up. "No, you're not. That other woman has taken over, so I can rest awhile. Wouldn't you like some tea?" she then queried.

"Only if you'll make a cup for yourself, too, Lady. I know you must be tired. Sorry I can't make the tea for both of us."

"You know, you're the only man I ever met who cared about any woman's being too tired," she volunteered, and her face softened a little. Then she called loudly, "Come here!" Soon-hee soon opened the door and put her head inside. "Make two cups of that persimmon drink the Ahn-Teacher liked so well the last time he was here," she ordered.

"Happily," Soon-hee responded and closed the door.

"She means well, Ahn-Teacher, but she's so young. What does she know about raising children? I suppose, of course there were younger children in her parents' family that she had to help with. But she goes about her work as if she enjoyed it! As if it were fun!"

The door suddenly popped open again. Soon-hee brought in the tray with the drinks which she must have had almost ready. Then she left.

Wun-yung's Mother continued with her tirade, "We need someone to work hard around here. How can you work hard while you're laughing? You know, I think that sometimes she's really trying to make me laugh, too. Ahn Teacher, if we both are laughing all the time, how would we ever get anything done around here?" Wun-yung's Mother complained.

"Well," Ahn answered, as he accepted his cup, "she certainly did **this** job in record time. I simply can't believe it. But, of course you are right, Wun-yung's Honorable Mother. How embarrassing it would be not to have most of your housework done when the hard-working Outside Lord* gets home from the fields. You wouldn't have any time to spend with him and the children if you hadn't finished your duties.

"You have additional help now, Wun-yung's Honorable Mother. You should have more time to rest and enjoy life with your nice family," Ahn suggested. "What do you think?"

"Yes, I know. It looks like it should be that way. But to tell you the truth, after we finish the dinner dishes, and stoke the awn-dawl fire, it's time for the younger children to go to bed. By then the Outside Lord is so sleepy, he's no company at all. And to be really honest, I'm pretty tired and drowsy myself. And I'm so far behind on the sewing, I don't think I'll ever get caught up," First-Wife concluded.

"Ha-ha-ha" Ahn broke out in a hearty, spontaneous laugh. "Please excuse me, but you remind me of our American saying, 'Man works from sun to sun; woman's work is never done.' "

Soon-hee, with Fourth on her back, was working in the kitchen. Now she reappeared to ask Wun-yung's Mother about plans for the evening meal. After discussing the meal, she backed out the door and stepped into her shoes. Ahn said, "Wait a minute, Soon-hee-ssee; you'll enjoy this. Do you know what Wun-yung's Honorable Mother needs more than anything else?

"It's a manager! Someone to tell her when to stop working, when to rest, when to play with the baby, when to read a fun book, when to take a little walk around the village and visit with some of the neighbors.

"Today, let's pretend I'm a doctor. I'm prescribing medicine and treatment for Wun-yung's Honorable Mother. And Soon-hee-ssee, you're the logical one to be the manager, so I'm appointing you. Now don't laugh! You heard what she said about laughing too much! But this is very serious. A whole family depends for its future and place-in-the-world on this being done right!

"Wun-yung's a big boy now. He can help with a lot more of the work around the home. Let one of his family chores be stoking fires before he settles down for his homework. When Wun-yung has to prepare for an examination the next day, let Tool-jjae have the fun of stoking. Doctor Ahn has spoken!"

Soon-hee smiled and withdrew. At that precise moment, the older boys rushed across the courtyard. Close behind them was Kee-haw, who couldn't wait another hour to come home. "I heard some strong talk coming from our house as I came down the lane. Tell me all about it. But first, Ahn-Mawk-sah, see what you think of my plan.

"The two boys are home and if you agree, they can spread the word over town. This is Wednesday evening. What better day for a Mid-week Service right here in Moo-jee-moo! We've got a preacher to preach. We'll borrow mats and cover the courtyard floor, and there will be room for the whole village, if they want to come. The only catch is that you will have to spend the night with us, for it will be too late to walk home afterwards."

"Kee-haw-ssee, you're a genius! Where do you get all these ideas? Maybe you are a mind-reader, because on the way out here I was wondering if Moo-jee-moo weren't about ready for a simple evangelistic meeting.

"There are probably quite a few who have had their curiosity piqued and who would come, if it were right here. They wouldn't have to lose almost a day going to the Eup*," Ahn agreed. "Yes, and the front porch of this house will make a perfect platform. Of course, we only have your hymnbook and mine and a few of the Mark-Good-News books that I brought with me. I only hope that Wun-yung's Honorable Mother doesn't mind putting up Dr. Ahn for the night. Ha-ha-ha!" Then turning to her, "You'll have to tell him about that!" Ahn chortled.

"I know, you two have been having jokes, but we'll have to save that 'Doctor-stuff' for later. Right now Wun-yung and Tool-jjae must run around to every house in this village and invite everyone to come tonight. And I have got to borrow lots of mats from the neighbors, besides tending to the livestock. We certainly don't want a cow moo-o-o-oing during the meeting in Moo-jee-moo! Ahn Mawk-sah told me that one!"

All joined in the laugh that followed. Even Kee-haw laughed at his own joke, then asked, "Soon-hee will you start a light supper for everyone and feed little Wun-bawg-ee? This will give Wun-yung's Mother some time to tidy up the front porch. She will want it to look neat when the town-folk come this evening."

During this time, Wun-yung and Tool-jjae had listened attentively. Now Tool-jjae offered his request, "Dad, please write out a piece of paper telling about this wonderful meeting. That will make it look much more important. If anyone wants to ask more questions, then Wun-yung and I will try to answer them. Wouldn't it be nice to tell them the time, too? We wouldn't want them coming before we're ready, would we?"

"No, that wouldn't bother me at all. If anyone comes early, I'll put him or her to work, helping me spread the mats. But I like your idea, Tool-jjae-yah. Let's circulate a friendly announcement. Give me a few minutes to mix the ink* and write the Koong-moon* carefully. We want it to look professional and artistic."

The minute Soon-hee heard the returning boys' voices outside the Great-Gate, she began serving up their rice and soup and one small dish of kim-chee* for both. The rest of the family had somehow managed to get in a few bites between different jobs that seemed important. Over half the mah-dahng* was already covered with mats and others were arriving every few minutes.

Ahn asked Kee-haw to take a short break to discuss plans for the order of the service and what he should include. "You are not a baptized-Christian as yet," he said, "but you understand the villagers much better than I. After all, this meeting is for them."

They decided quickly that there should be no offering. Kee-haw and Ahn knew "Jesus Loves Me," so they would sing two stanzas of that.

Ahn agreed to ask the crowd to sing the chorus once or twice. He hoped there were enough Good News books so that each literate adult could use one.

Before long a few earlybirds started arriving. As Paek had expected they were glad to shed their too-roo-mah-gee*, roll up their sleeves and help bring in and spread mats. Paek introduced each family to Ahn Pastor before he set the men to work.

Ahn had been helping Paek until this help came. Now he desisted, knowing that the more the villagers put themselves into the meeting, the more they would get from it. Quite a few children, having heard from the two boys of the unusual evening affair, drifted in. They stood around the edges, often helping when they saw a chance.

In another half-hour, every mat was filled with people. A few timid souls stood inside the Great-Gate against the wall on each side. Kee-haw gave the prearranged signal and Ahn started in. He wanted to make the meeting as simple as possible, yet still get the important truths across. He would keep it reasonably short, knowing the parents would be more willing to come again, and the school children would get their sleep.

Singing "Jesus Loves Me," only brought a few smothered grins from the teenagers and some of the women. Very few tried to join in the chorus. Ahn asked those who could read to raise their hands. Fortunately there were enough copies of the Gospel of Mark to go around. He asked them to find Mark

12:29-31, so they could follow the reading of the Great God of Heaven's word to them.

"Part of God's Holy Words are in your hands. Usually I sell these Good News books for the cost price to whoever wants them. But tonight you have been very kind to come out in the cold air. So I am going to offer each of you who reads, a gift of an important part of God's holy word. Each of you may keep the little book that is in your hand. Please accept this gift."

Then the missionary read slowly the great summation of God's perfect will for mankind. When he finished he said, "Some of you people of Moo-jee-moo are very friendly. In time I trust that all of you will be. God loves every single one of you. Yes, even that tiny baby who can't talk yet and is carried on his mother's back and the old grandfather who has to have three legs to walk.

"In my country, we say the noise a cow makes is 'moo.' This afternoon, one Moo-jee-moo citizen said, 'I don't want a hungry cow mooing in Moo-jee-moo's first Christian meeting.' I realize it's an English pun, but I like it, don't you? Anyway, notice how quiet the cattle in this neighborhood are at this hour. They're not hungry anymore. They're all fed. Are you hungry for God's great truths? Please don't answer, 'Moo-oo-oo!' That would not be appropriate. But joking aside, we have read some of the greatest of God's truths together this evening, and we have found that the first and greatest commandment God has given men is, 'Love God with all your heart and soul and mind and strength.' The second greatest is, 'Love others as much as you love yourself.'

"Now I'm going to ask a question of each of you, not just those who are holding books. Do you love Hah-nah-nim that much? With all your heart and soul and mind and strength? Look into your heart. Do you truly and honestly think, way down deep in your innermost heart, that you are obeying God's greatest commandment? Most of your families now have a copy of God's Word. If any of you don't, I'll bring some more next time. Study God's Word. Those who can read, read it out loud to those who can't. If some of you older folks have to listen to some of your school children reading, that's fine too. These books contain God's Way and God's Truth and God's Life.

"Especially, they tell about Jesus, the only Son of Hah-nah-nim, who, to demonstrate God's love, came to earth, to live as a man among men and lead us back to Hah-nah-nim. A few minutes ago, I gave you some Good News books. God gave us his One and Only Son. Why? By His death on a cross, to save us from sins and to make us His good children. Why did he die? So He could be our Savior!

"How do we become God's forgiven children? How do our lives become so changed that we live in daily fellowship with Him? By simply changing the direction we are going, by living with Christ as our Master, by being sorry for our sins and accepting Jesus's death for us. Speaking very plainly, this means accepting Jesus as the One who saves us, our Savior. Anyone who takes this step, thereby becomes a Christ-Person or Christian. And the Spirit of God lives in him, stays with him and leads him the rest of his life. Can you possibly imagine any greater Salvation?

"I am going to pass on to you some Words that God has spoken. He has spoken them to each one of us; He is speaking them now to you. I wish I could write them in letters of shining fire on the sky, where you could see them every moment of the day and night. These Words of God are: 'Do not neglect so great a salvation!'

"If God has been speaking to any of you this evening, inside your hearts, and telling you, personally, not to neglect so great a salvation I'm going to give you a chance to let us know by raising your hand. I will be glad to talk to you after the meeting, answer any questions, and explain to you what you should do next.

"Let us bow our heads for the closing prayer. Now, while our eyes are closed, please raise your hands if you want Christ to be your own Savior, and you want me to pray to God our Father especially for you."

In God's quiet but pervasive way, Kee-haw had been finding that his life needed the sovereignty of the only One who knew the beginning and the end. He had decided that very day, while alone out in his fields, that there was no other Name under heaven by which he could be saved! He was thankful for the opportunity to express this decision so soon. Quickly he held up his hand. Several others followed.

When everyone had finally gone home and most of the mats had been taken home with them, Kee-haw and Ahn were having a night-cap of two small cups of barley-tea. Kee-haw thanked the missionary for his willingness to stay overnight, especially since he hadn't really planned on it. Ahn explained to Kee-haw that since there was no telephone as yet in Moo-jee-moo, he and his wife had an agreement. The last words he had said to his Inside Woman* when he left the house, were, "Expect me when you see me. I may be home this evening, but I'll try to be flexible. Perhaps the Lord will want me to stay over and hold an Evening Service."

Kee-haw responded: "My, it must be wonderful to know that God is in charge of everything. Then you can accept whatever comes as His will. Any non-Christian woman with that much uncertainty would worry until her husband turned up. He might even be dead-drunk in a ditch somewhere, catching his death of cold. But I did want to ask you about the Service this evening. What was your impression?"

"Well, Kee-haw-ssee, I felt that though almost everyone in the village came, sheer curiosity brought too many of them. I sensed a lot of opposition, though maybe not open hostility, as if they were thinking, 'He's just a foreigner. What does he know about our ways, our religion, what suits us?' Let's just say that a lot of the villagers seemed to have a basic unwillingness to really settle down and think seriously and deeply about the major life issues involved.

"In other words, too many came to see a show, and being in that spirit, they got a show, and not too good a one at that. Now I know this is very negative, and we, as followers of the Christ, must keep our minds centered on Him and His positive truth. Hah-nah-nim's Spirit was working. There's no doubt of that; and we should be very deeply grateful!

"A few of those who stayed afterwards were more concerned about non-essentials and were still motivated by a certain amount of curiosity. Still, God's Spirit broke through at least some of the barriers, and in time, we trust, will win out. We must support this work of the Spirit in our 'fervent effectual prayers.' Please tell your son Wun-yung that his prayers can be just as effective as ours, or even more so."

For the next four or five months, Kee-haw, quite faithfully, made the 30 lee round-trip to the city every Sunday. Maw-see-paht, the county seat, or Eup, where the church was located, seemed far from home, except on market days. Then he found many others on the road with whom to talk. But there was no closer Meeting Place, and because Ahn and Lee were always friendly and cordial, Kee-haw never felt he was imposing on them. He felt sure that their pleasure in seeing and chatting with him was genuine.

If they had other appointments, they would frankly tell him. Otherwise they invited him to their homes for a cup of some delicious drink. This gave him time, fairly often, to let them catch up on news of his private life as well as his progress in The Faith.

The first few week-ends, Kee-haw admitted to himself, he too had made the trip partly out of curiosity. He resented the long hike, the time wasted from his fields and the extra wear on his home-made straw-shoes. But by the second month, he found that this new Jesus-teaching gave him a weekly boost and was almost like a tonic. At least the first three days of every week were far easier than they used to be, and for some reason Sour-face didn't seem to be so sour!

Kee-haw knew that somehow a portion of the Inner Peace was gradually seeping through to him. He wondered sometimes if it could be going past him into Wun-yung's Mother. Of course, it sounded rather ridiculous on the surface. "But," he said to himself, "it's what goes on underneath that really matters."

He began not to mind the long walk and the loss of time, he noticed that he looked forward to the weekly trip. He began to tell people along the way about this new discovery. Of course, he did not mention the problems of his own family life. But, though it seemed a bit strange, he knew for a fact, and gladly shared with others, that his farm work hadn't suffered. On the contrary, it even seemed to be doing better.

Now he wasn't trying to cram in a whole day's work before the two o'clock afternoon worship service. He was getting up earlier that he used to, even for a farmer, and getting all his chores done around the house even more efficiently. Of course, Wun-yung was getting older and was able to help him more. But the wonder of it was that for the last two months, Soon-hee had been packing lunches for three. She was even joining him and Wun-yung in getting there for the ten o'clock Bible Class. Soon-hee also left nice lunches for the other four of the family who stayed home, so Wun-yung's Mom couldn't complain.

When church was over they chatted with the ministers. Then they hiked home. It was always five or after, and they arrived home famished. However, Kee-haw knew that his inside hunger was being filled.

Soon-hee seemed even happier than before. Only occasionally did he catch a half-pensive, half-wistful look in her eyes. Kee-haw had, however, almost given up trying to get First-Wife to go with them on Sunday morning, even though he was positive now that this Jesus-teaching was the only thing that would help her remove that sour look and live at peace under her roof.

When he was home, she didn't even seem to act as though he was there. Many times, when he tried to speak kindly, she didn't answer. In his more quiet times, he wondered if she really wanted to be separated from all others. More frequently she encouraged Soon-hee to carry Fourth on her back as she worked. Thus, First-Wife wouldn't have to worry about watching him to see that he didn't hurt himself about the house.

It seemed that February would never come to an end. The last snow was finally all melted, except on the higher peaks of the nearby mountains. Even though March was just around the corner, somehow no one in the family had foreseen the dramatic changes which this spring season of new life would bring.

CHAPTER IX
Soon-hee Is Pregnant

One Sunday, early in March, the grandmother-flower* buds were opening on the hills and on some of the rice-paddy un-duk*. Kee-haw woke up bright and early. Without disturbing Soon-hee, he slipped out quietly and tended to the feeding of the farm animals. Usually Soon-hee was up, dressed and busy, by the time he got back. But this time, the cottage was strangely quiet. First-Wife was grumbling as usual in the kitchen . . . or was it more than usual? But the funny thing was, she seemed to be alone.

Quickly he jerked open the door with the little glass pane. There was his Soon-hee, still under the covers on the floor. He could sense that she was trying hard to be her usual, cheerful self, but her success was certainly nothing to pass on to future generations! "It seems like it's an inside sickness," she volunteered, "but I can't understand because my head aches, too!"

Kee-haw kneeled on the oil-paper floor, so he wouldn't have to shed his shoes, reached across and patted her head: "Don't worry, Paw-bae-yah, you'll feel better soon. I'll stoke up the fire under the floor, so the room will be warm all day. You'd better not try to go to church today. Maybe you have a cold."

Later he carried her some hot broth from the big-house kitchen. "Look, my Beauty," he said, "Wun-yung and I must start soon, but please be careful of your health today. If Wun-yung wants to stay there and play with his friends, he can. Of course, he will take a lunch with him and attend the afternoon Service. But I'll come home after the Bible Class. In the meantime, I've told First-Wife she'd better take good care of you or else . . ."

Soon-hee smiled and chuckled: "Don't worry, sweet Hubby. Before long I'll be myself, and then nobody will need to take care of me. Run along and remember every single word, so you can teach me the lesson when you get back."

Kee-haw was becoming very fond and a bit proud of his "First-born Rascal." Wun-yung had been going to Sunday School and Church with him for five or six months. Kee-haw could see a rapid growth in understanding and comprehension on Wun-yung's part. Kee-haw daily thanked God for this and prayed that soon Tool-jjae, the Second, would be able to take the long Sunday hikes.

Today, without Soon-hee along, Kee-haw could give Wun-yung his full attention. It was a rewarding experience for both of them. "Ah-bu-jee (Father)," Wun-yung began, "aren't we losing income for our family by not going to Sunday markets any more? I don't believe you've gone for the last three months, have you? What do you think, Ah-bu-jee?"

"Well, son, you can be sure that I've thought very seriously about that, especially when I first decided it wasn't right. You see, God only asks us for one-seventh of our days and one-tenth of our income, which is very generous. Of course he expects us to live good, clean, Christian lives every day. He also expects us to use all our money wisely so it will bring Him glory or praise. But He expressly asked us not to work on Sunday. And loading the grain onto the cow, leading it to market and bartering there for a good price, is a lot of hard work. If you don't believe me, come to market some time when you have a holiday, and see how I sweat in that hot sun and dust.

"So I said to myself, 'There are lots of nice people in that Church who are not starving to death, even though they don't work on Sundays. If they can do it, I can, too!' And then, Wun-yung, I said to God, 'Look, God, everything we have comes from you and is really yours. We just use it for awhile. You are Almighty, All Powerful. If you want our income to come to us on six days instead of seven, that's easy for you to arrange. I'll just take my hands off and give you complete freedom to provide any way you please.'

"Following my talk with God, I just said, 'Ah-men.' And that sort of sealed the deal. It was kind of like stamping it with my taw-jahng*, you know. Since God had told us that's what He wanted us to do, and we were doing it, it had to work. And I'm glad to report to you that it has been working. Why, someone told me the other day that in some countries every Saturday is also a holiday, so they only work and go to school five days a week!"

"Dad, don't you think that maybe we learn more on Sundays than we do on any other day?" Wun-yung queried again.

"It's hard to measure such things, son. Of course, it makes a difference whether you're talking about quantities that you can measure in human ways and maybe see with your eyes, or not. But if you're talking about true values that last forever, I would answer, 'Yes, most certainly.' " Then, after a short pause, Kee-haw continued, "Son, I'm proud of you. You're doing some solid thinking."

Once more, Wun-yung looked backward and forward to be sure no one was within ear-shot. Then he ventured a question, "Dad, what do we do when we make wrong decisions before we know they are wrong?"

Kee-haw sensed what was coming, but countered by asking two questions of his own: "Can you be more precise? How about an example?"

"Well, look at our family, Dad. My Sunday School teacher told us that polygamy is not right for Christians, even though it was allowed thousands of years ago in Old Testament times. But you married Kim Soon-hee before you knew that. That's what I mean."

"Son, in my blindness and ignorance, I followed the dictates of my own selfish thinking and a very dear friend's advice. At first, looking at it in this way, we rationalized that it would be better for everyone involved, including your mother. However, actually son, to tell you the honest truth, we never considered whether it would be better for Soon-hee-ssee or not. That would have interfered with my selfish thinking, you see.

"Even before the missionary first came to visit, I wondered if I had been wrong. Now, I am working day and night to find some solution that will hurt everyone the least, everyone that is except myself. As God is leading me in my thinking, Wun-yung, it seems inevitable that I will be hurt the most. Maybe this is because in the first place I was thinking most selfishly of my own needs. Of course, this is my own idea, and maybe in time God can help me to see otherwise. But why, my son, do you think I spend so much time in conference with Lee Mawk-sah and Ahn Mawk-sah? It is not just for fun, son. You can depend on that."

Then after a few moments when only their footsteps were heard, he added, "Son, I want to thank you for being so frank and candid. This is not always easy between father and son, but, please, let's always have it that way between us."

After Sunday School that morning, Wun-yung hunted up his dad. He asked permission to go home with a friend from the class for an hour or so. He said this friend's dad was an elder in the church, so he was sure it was a nice home.

Kee-haw replied, "Sure, that's fine, Wun-yung-ee. But just remember, with Soon-hee-ssee sick, I'm not staying for the afternoon Worship Service today. I'm going up to Ahn Mawk-sah's for a short talk with him. When you get through at your friend's, come there. Be careful of your lunch. Maybe Ahn Mawk-sah will let you eat in his lovely yard, or on the hill behind his house. Then if you want to join your friend again for the Church Service, all right. If not, you can come home with me, whichever you'd prefer."

"Thank you, Honorable Father, I'll see you in an hour or so," Wun-yung answered and ran to catch up with his friend.

Kee-haw turned his steps toward the Mission Compound. For several Sundays he had missed seeing Ahn Pastor at the main church. As he had heard nothing of any illness, he had assumed that the missionary had started his spring itineration. Or else he could be visiting some struggling nearby church.

So Kee-haw was all the more happy that he had seen him at Sunday School this morning. After Sunday School he had made sure that this was a convenient time to drop by.

"Many apologies for not coming to see you sooner, Ahn Mawk-sah," Kee-haw greeted him. "Since I haven't been seeing you at Church, I figured you must be out of town. And several Sundays, for some reason or other, I've been in a hurry to get home myself. How have things been going with you and the thirty-five churches which have been assigned to you?"

"Oh, pretty good, thank you, Kee-haw-ssee. But my very special friend, tell me, how are things in your family? That's what I can't wait to hear."

"Well, I won't keep you waiting a minute longer, my friend from another world! For awhile, after your second visit, and the evening meeting at our home, things seemed to be somewhat better. We could go for quite a few days, almost a week, without any noticeable friction. It was quite evident that Soon-hee was doing her part to take over certain jobs or duties. Thus Wun-yung's Mother could relax and rest, or do things she really enjoyed doing. And Soon-hee has practically taken over the mending and sewing, so we're completely caught up there.

"But I can't say that Wun-yung's Mother's disposition or attitude toward life in general or toward the children and me has really changed. Oh, Ahn Mawk-sah, I had so hoped that by this visit there would be some definite improvement to report. Then this would have been a pleasant visit!"

"Human relations are complex at best, my wonderful friend," Ahn replied.

"I just can't tell you how much I appreciate your coming back all the way to Moo-jee-moo that second time, and your talking with Wun-yung's Mother, and holding the Evangelistic Service right in our own yard, Ahn Mawk-sah! I just happened to think of something. Do you suppose she heard something at the meeting that touched her? Maybe that's why she hasn't continued to get worse, as she was doing previously?" Kee-haw asked.

"But, good friend," Kee-haw went on, "I wanted to bring you up to date on the definite results of the meeting. I'm so happy to tell you the Lord has looked on us with favor and blessing. Out of those who stayed for awhile after the meeting, three men are coming to my sah-rahng* every Wednesday evening. I'm trying to pass on to them everything I remember from the previous Sunday's Bible lesson and sermon. That is at least as much as they seem to be able to absorb.

"And there's another man who is coming as well. You'll never guess who he is! It's Wun-sik, my lifelong friend! It won't be too long, I'm sure, until all four will be strong enough to come with me to Sunday School and Church! How does that sound to you, friend from another world?" Kee-haw finished.

"Oh, Kee-haw-ssee, I'm so excited! Isn't that marvelous! Our God is still the God of miracles! And remember, the Meeting was your idea! See how God is using you already!" Then Ahn rather abruptly changed from the excited, jovial friend to the solemn and sober one. He turned and faced Kee-haw squarely. "I missed Soon-hee-ssee this morning and as yet you haven't said one word about her. Where is she?" he asked, concern written all over his face.

"Oh, she was not well, so I had her remain lying down," Kee-haw quickly answered.

Ahn raised his eyebrows, "You mean it came on early this morning?"

Kee-haw chuckled knowingly, "Well, y.e.e.s.s. it was early all right! Rising time is always early, Mawk-sah, on Sundays, even more so than on other days. But I really think it's only a cold this time. Save your congratulations for later!" Both men laughed heartily, but almost instantaneously Kee-haw's face resumed the former worried look.

"Mawk-sah, things are gradually getting worse in several ways. I'm sure of this; too many people are being hurt. And how can I teach God's Word to anyone, when I myself am not obeying and living by it? God does not do things this way! What can I do?" Kee-haw queried, obviously troubled.

After remaining still for several moments, Ahn said, "Kee-haw-ssee, prayer is the greatest force on earth. Don't underestimate it. First, we will continue to pray, all of us. Next time Soon-hee-ssee comes with you, drop in again. Surely God will show us what is best. You may get the answer before I do. You'd better go back to her now."

A month or more later, on a particularly bright spring noon after the morning Bible Classes, Soon-hee, Kee-haw and Wun-yung took their lunches up on the back hill, behind the Meeting Place. There they had a pleasant picnic. The hill was all that remained of the old city wall of a thousand years ago. Digging around could still yield lovely artifacts in perfect condition*.

They had brought their balls of crisp rice. Some of it was browned for more flavor and wrapped up in a clean cloth. After lunch, Kee-haw said, "Let's take a walk." They then followed the hill, made by men and the elements, around to the west edge of town and back again.

Before coming down from the hill, Kee-haw spoke to Wun-yung, "Son, do you have any friends you'd like to spend an hour or so with this afternoon? I mean after the Church Service? Soon-hee-ssee and I need to have a talk with Ahn Mawk-sah."

"Sure, Dad; no problem. There are the nicest young folks in this Church. They're always asking me to come and play at their homes for awhile. Where will I meet you?"

"If your friends live out on the east side of town, why don't you meet us where we ford the river?" Kee-haw answered.

"That's perfect!" Wun-yung agreed.

It wasn't long until the two o'clock Service, so they went back to the Church, Wun-yung running ahead of the two adults. After the Service, Kee-haw said to Soon-hee, "Paw-bae-yah, I'm so glad we're going to have a chance to see Ahn-Pastor today. Thank you for suggesting it. He seems to understand so many things far better than we, even though he is a foreigner and rather young. It will make us somewhat late getting home, and Sour-face will doubtless explode! But we need to think out loud with someone who cares, don't we?"

"Yes, my dear husband; we always feel so much better after we do. We can put up with the yah-dahn* again, I'm sure."

So following the Service, they went up to Ahn Pastor's study. A neatly dressed Korean woman, wearing an apron, ushered them in. Soon Ahn entered. Genuine pleasure showed on his face and in his voice, "Oh-h-h-h, I'm so glad you stayed awhile. I should have asked you long ago whether coming to talk at this hour upsets Wun-yung's Honorable Mother or not. If it does, we could work out some earlier hour, I'm sure."

Kee-haw and Soon-hee both burst out in a spontaneous laugh. As soon as he got control, Kee-haw apologized, "Excuse our unseemly mirth, good friend from another world. Not fifteen minutes ago, Soon-hee and I were talking about that very subject. I was commenting that there would probably be a yah-dahn when we got home this afternoon. You see, we'll be later then usual. Isn't that funny? How could all three of us be thinking the same thing at the same time!

"You know, Soon-hee and I are Christians now and we believe that God can help us in our thinking, if we ask him to, but many non-Christians think that our sorceresses can read what people are thinking by magic. Do you think this is possible, Honorable Mawk-sah?"

"Well, Kee-haw-ssee," Ahn replied, "some scientists at Duke University have conducted experiments. And they have found that some people are much more psychic than others. They call it having extrasensory perception, E.S.P. Maybe that's what makes your sorceresses different from other people!

"But tell me about yourselves and your sweet family and your Wednesday evening group. It's really hard for me to get along without news of you and Moo-jee-moo."

"Nothing really new, Honorable Ahn Mawk-sah," Kee-haw spoke up. "Sometimes it seems as though the old relation with First Wife gets even worse. You will remember that you warned both of us, even from the beginning, that our lot would not be easy. You have more wisdom than your years, sir. It is extremely difficult for each of the three of us adults. In some respects, even the children have felt the strain in the air. What shall we do, Ahn Mawk-sah?"

Thoughtfully, slowly and rather wisely, Ahn gave his reply. "God does not ask us to be responsible for all the things which in our ignorance we did before we knew Him, my friends. The King of Heaven came to teach us to live together in Peace. True Peace, however, cannot be had at the expense of another's misfortune. What is truly good for one, must be truly good for all. Of course, we have hoped and prayed that your First-Wife would find whatever Peace she needs. The Jesus Teachings and Way of Life should bring this. But she has not accepted them yet.

"Each person is an individual, which simply means that each person's response to God's invitation is different. If Wun-yung's Honorable Mother had found Peace in God, it seems to me that God would give the mutual understanding needed for whatever lies ahead. However, our Heavenly Father may have some other more satisfactory solution. We will keep praying for this. But has anything else occurred to you, my friends?"

Kee-haw replied, "I tell Soon-hee that First-Wife is very healthy and may live for many, many years. At first, when we didn't know any better, we assumed that the triangle relation would be possible. In fact, it seemed to have been proven possible through the centuries in our land. But now, with added insight, we feel quite sure that Soon-hee could never be entirely happy as a ch'up, a Second-Wife.

"We do not like to think about this, Honorable Mawk-sah. It is much easier in our minds to run away from the problem and only live from one day to the next with our great joy in being together. But, nevertheless, we know that what I am saying is true. Soon-hee's children can never have full legal status, and even a woman does not always want to be under someone else's authority."

Soon-hee vigorously nodded her head up and down in oriental agreement.

"Moreover, I am a Christian, and whether Christian or not, First-Wife has borne me three fine sons and a sweet daughter. What shall I do, Ahn Mawk-sah? I should be the scandal of the country if I took the other alternative and divorced her."

Soon-hee took advantage of a slight pause to say softly but vehemently, "Oh no, no, no; that could never be." Then she looked coyly at Ahn and volunteered, "A month or more ago, my husband told me that you two were joking about my morning indisposition. You remember I didn't accompany him to the Eup, that Sunday morning. Honorable Ahn Mawk-sah, I consider my husband to be a pretty smart man, though maybe not as smart as you. However, that day, you were smarter than he."

"Well then, immediately and without further ado, let me congratulate both of you from the depths of my heart," Ahn replied with radiant face. "How happy you must be!"

"Thank you, Honorable Mawk-sah," Kee-haw resumed. "How thoughtful you are! Yes, truly we are supremely happy, even though it has not meant any diminishing of our many problems. But as you know, Ahn Mawk-sah, even though I have almost finished reading clear through my Bible twice, I cannot feel that God's Word allows the divorce of my First-Wife. Thousands of years ago, perhaps it might have been permitted. And at that stage of human development, perhaps, I would not have been as concerned about Soon-hee's welfare. But even then, First-Wife's children would have been my children, and I don't see how I could not think of them."

After a long pause in which Kee-haw was evidently thinking deeply, he said, "There is only one solution, Honorable Mawk-sah. We must find a good Christian husband for Soon-hee. She must be a First-Wife, not a Second."

Soon-hee's head dropped forward. The tears were coming fast. It was the missionary pastor who spoke now, very gently. Using the honorable suffix on her name, he said, "Soon-hee-ssee, I know you don't want to leave this man who loves you so and whom you love so much. In order to do the right thing by you, he is not even considering himself and his own happiness!

"But don't you feel that your husband is right? Is there not someone that is not too young, or who possibly has lost his wife and who of course is a Christian? With him you might find this true and undivided love that every woman needs." Soon-hee was sobbing as if her heart would break.

Ahn went on, "I, too, believe that God wants you to have this, Soon-hee-ssee. This is your husband's true love that is speaking. If I might paraphrase Another's unforgettable Words, I would say, 'Greater love hath no man than this, that a man lay down his own happiness, which is really his life, for his friend.' "

Soon-hee made no attempt to hide her tears. The two men could see very plainly that her emotions were completely real, and that she was not ashamed of them. Nor would she ever be, come what might. They were hers, a very part of her, just as much as her hands or her delicate ears. Her open and genuine expression of her feelings brought understanding and respect from the two men.

Now she swept aside her inborn, oriental modesty as she looked Ahn right in the eyes. "The good God of Heaven has sent you clear across the ocean to us, Ahn Mawk-sah, for just this moment in our troubled lives," she said. "That which I want, and I believe my husband wants, more than anything else, is to spend our lives together. I never saw such an unselfish and thoughtful man in all my life and have no desire or intention to look for another.

"You talk about 'this true and undivided love that every woman needs.' I already have that love. Why should I give it up? Why should I look for another? What is going to become of me and of my husband's child and mine, without a husband and father? There is no other man who can be half as kind and unselfish as he, or ever take his place! There are too many angles in this triangular family to be settled so easily."

Soon-hee had thought through what she was saying many times in the last few weeks. But now, the very act of saying it in the presence of her husband and an understanding and loving friend broke something loose within her. The tears, too, broke loose afresh. She paused as deep sobs wracked her from head to foot and took control for several minutes.

Wiping some of her tears away with both hands, Soon-hee resumed her defense. But now there was something different. Her love had taken on greater proportions. She was not a lone woman, fighting against the whole world for her birthright, the love of one man. She knew she had that love and did not want to give it up.

Deep within her, the knowledge was growing that in a certain sense, in addition to being one woman, she was speaking for womankind of all ages!

Could it possibly be that the Great God of Heaven, Who spared not His only Son, was honoring her also with a **certain crucifixion** that would redound to His honor and **serve all humankind** BY EXAMPLE?

Soft elements of spirit-healing had already begun to replace the harder lines of severe suffering in her expressive face. Somehow the missionary was able to sense some of the resolution of the conflict. Hesitantly, but very tenderly, he spoke, "Soon-hee-ssee and Kee-haw-ssee, man's happiness and the laws of God are one and the same because they are not imposed on us; they are rather, part of us. They are written in our bones and flesh, in the fiber of our beings. We cannot really break those laws.

"Let's imagine that a man steps off the roof of a high tile-roofed house. He does not break the law of gravity, but his failure to observe the law breaks him. In blissful ignorance and selfishness, you two failed to observe an important law of God. Many people have felt at least part of the breaking that has resulted. Now that you know better, you will do better. Happiness will result, for you will be with and in the laws of God and man."

"Oh, Honorable Ahn Mawk-sah," Soon-hee almost interrupted, "do you think this is really possible? A moment ago I saw myself on a cross making a sacrifice of all that which is most dear to me. Might I thus find myself in a greater fulfillment of a **GREATER LOVE** that brought hurt to no one?

Do you think that the Great God of the universe would stoop to honor me with such a favor?"

"Yes, Soon-hee-ssee, God has been talking to you directly. I could see some of it written on your face. Jesus told all of us to take up our crosses and follow Him. A cross means crucifixion. Yes, God, in His mercy, has honored you above many, and you have heard him and understood. God bless you both."

The conference ended very shortly. Wun-yung met them at the appointed place, and all three headed for home.

CHAPTER X
A Possible New Husband

Later in the evening, after the three younger children had gone to sleep, Kee-haw and Soon-hee retired to their one room and lean-to cottage. Kee-haw had a comforting thought, a famous saying of the great scholar*. "Soon-hee Darling," he began, "this is not from the Bible, but it's a wonderful saying, just the same: 'When Heaven is about to confer a great office on any man, it first exerts his mind with suffering.'* Doesn't that give a lift to your spirit, Sweetie? It surely does mine."

"Oh, you dear husband," Soon-hee answered, "just when I needed it the most, you bring forth this gem! How it sparkles with hope! What marvelous thing, what 'great office' do you suppose lies ahead of us? she asked.

"You know, of course, my father and mother are not Christians as yet, though I pray daily that God will somehow reveal the light to them; several years ago, father somewhere ran across an old saying of the Honorable Confucius*: 'Virtue is not left to stand alone. He who practices it will have neighbors*.' It meant so much to all our family! Let's put the two proverbs together and remember them forever, with our new Jesus-Way teachings."

"Changing the subject, Paw-bae-yah, yesterday, I had a nice chat with my best friend, Wun-sig-ee. You know, he's the one who helped me build our home and arranged with your father for our marriage. He might come over for awhile this evening, if he can finish up his chores in time. I really haven't had a chance to visit with him properly for ever so long. When we don't have time for our best friends, what happens to all the rest of them? Do you have anything in our kitchen over here that we could fix up quickly for a nice drink for the three of us, Paw-bae-yah?"

Soon-hee, bright and cheerful as usual, came over to Kee-haw, who was already sitting on the "hot-spot," closest to the kitchen. Kee-haw took her hand and gently pulled her down toward him. She had been trying to take a sitting position in front of him. But his pull was too strong and before she quite knew what was happening, she lost her balance and fell rather awkwardly into his lap.

Both Kee-haw's arms quickly encircled her and pulled her very close. "Oh, Paw-bae-yah," he said, as laughingly she nestled even closer, "how am I ever going to live all the rest of my life without your laughter in my ears, your fresh, clean odor in my nose, your pure beauty in my eyes and your precious love in my heart?" Tears were streaming down his manly, suntanned cheeks. "Paw-bae-yah, will I ever smile again?"

Soon-hee's eyes, too, were brimming over, but she didn't give in to her emotions. Instead she straightened up, used the ever-present petticoat to clear her vision, stood up and said, "Look, sweet husband, we'll have time later, but your friend may be outside the Big-Gate right now and I'm not ready for . . . ." A series of loud yelps came from the courtyard as faithful Blackie announced the visitor.

Soon-hee dived through the kitchen door. Kee-haw jumped up, and very quickly grabbed a hand towel from the peg on the wall-post. He wiped his face and eyes, and while calling, "Yes, I'm going*," opened the paper-door and slipped into his straw-shoes. As he hurried across the courtyard, he had enough presence of mind to speak sharply to the dog and tell him to stop the din.

Wun-sik called through the Great-Gate to reassure Kee-haw, who then slid back the heavy wooden bolt. In the meanwhile, Blackie had retired behind the corner of the house. There the dog felt safe enough to let his nose protrude while he continued to bark.

"Come in! Come in!" Kee-haw welcomed his friend. "Where have you been hiding all these last hundred years, you rascal? Don't give me any silly excuses; you know perfectly well you've just been staying night and day on the other side of the mountain."

"Now, take it easy, you monster," Wun-sik came back, "you know it isn't that bad. Why it was only yesterday we had a nice chat over by Kim-Miller's place. Shame on you! I thought you were my friend! Why did I come all the way over here through those pitch-black lanes to see the likes of you? Go on back to your old house; see if I care!"

"Now you are going to make me mad, you rascal, calling this house that you helped me build an old house. Just for that, I'm going to get even with you." Kee-haw grabbed Wun-sik's arm and lowered his voice. "Just for that, you've got to come over here and greet the dragon in her lair. I told you I'd get even!"

Wun-sik had on his clean, long white robe or too-roo-mah-gee*. His hair was freshly cut and neatly brushed, and he entered right into the fun. In a short time, he turned the tables and was pulling Kee-haw to the Big-house. Quite firmly he spoke clearly, "Of course I must salute the Queen, Wun-yung's Honorable Mother. Do you think I came just to see you? Hah! You make me laugh."

To be very honest, First-Wife, with her supposedly morose disposition, was not in the habit of spending much time outside her own Great-Gate. Nor did she visit much with the other village women. And now that Soon-hee had taken over most of the laundry duties, she hadn't appeared at the stream where the big, flat scrubbing-stones were, for several months. Thus, when Wun-sik's imitation cough brought First-Wife to the main kitchen's outside door, Wun-sik's most natural greeting was, "It's been a long, long time since I last saw you."

First-Wife returned the greeting and wiped her hands on her clean, starched apron. She stepped over to the outside door of the sah-rahng, and opened it. "Please go in," she bowed. "It's nothing much to look at, but you are most welcome. Please sit over there where it's warm."

Wun-sik doffed his shoes, crossed the porch and entered the sah-rahng. As he passed Kee-haw, he heard him mutter under his breath, "Keu gut ch'ahm, (what do you know!) The floor's warm. Isn't that marvelous! How did she know you were coming?"

They both sat down, Wun-sik on the "hot-spot" and Kee-haw nearby. Kee-haw leaned over close to Wun-sik and in a voice muted almost to a whisper, he said, "Strange things are happening around here. Wun-yung's Mother never heats this floor unless I ask her to, or a guest is coming. She must have started the fire an hour or two ago, but how did she know you were coming? I only told Soon-hee five minutes ago!"

Wun-sik answered softly, "Don't ask me! Nothing surprises me any more! My Inside-Woman left this world last winter. And since I started coming to the Wednesday-night meetings, God has given me so many surprises. Of course, one of the best is when God used you to open Heaven's glories to me."

At that moment, the door whooshed open with something like a sucking noise. Sayt-jjae stepped in, quickly went to her knees and in her dainty way, bowed low to Wun-sik. Her mother followed close behind with a small, low table, on which were placed, as on a tray, several small cups of steaming barley-tea! "Another mystery!" thought Kee-haw. "How in the world, with no warning at all, had Wun-yung's Mother produced the refreshments in such a short time? And even a dish of several pieces of yut, or wheat-gluten candy, sprinkled with sesame seed. It took cash to buy such luxuries! Where had she gotten some cash, when he didn't even have a single p'oon of cash* to his name right now?"

First-Wife set the table within reach of both men. She first set a cup of hot tea on the edge of the table closest to each man. Then she picked up another cup and took it with her as she sat down a few feet away. She was close enough so the floor wasn't really cold.

The hot tea served more than one purpose on this chilly evening. Wun-sik opened the conversation. "Wun-yung's Honorable Mother, you know it's a shame that we have all our Wednesday-night meetings over in the other house. No one who attends can know how nicely you keep your part of the establishment. You are really an exceedingly fine housekeeper and others in Moo-jee-moo should know and appreciate this."

Such a well-worded compliment from such a nicely groomed gentleman was almost too much for First-Wife. In fact, she couldn't remember when she had heard a nicer one. Not in years had she blushed as she did just then. It took her so by surprise that she coughed a little on the tea, but she put the cup down on the oil-papered floor and bowed low to Wun-sik. "Ch'un mahn-ee mahl-sseum ee-awl-see-tah," or "You exaggerate ten million times," she responded.

Then after a moment she continued, "You know, it's a little strange, but we are all fortunate that we could use this room tonight. We don't have to sit in the somewhat untidy family room. You see, I wanted to cook an extra vegetable for tonight's meal because I knew that the three of them would be tired from the long day in the Eup and the walk there and back. That's how I happened to use the cooking pot that is suspended over the place where we build the fire to heat this floor. You may have thought that it was funny that this awn-dawl was warm."

"Yes, I was just telling Kee-haw that Heaven smiles on us when we least expect it. But isn't it fun to have those kinds of surprises? It really makes life more interesting, doesn't it?" Wun-sik contributed. "The God of Heaven is good to us all, whether we recognize it or not. It really would be kind of appropriate to say 'Thank You,' wouldn't it? You won't mind, will you, Wun-yung's Honorable Mother?"

"Oh no, it sounds good, but I don't know how," she answered.

"Just fold your hands like this," Wun-sik explained. "Most of us think it helps to close our eyes, thus shutting out other things, but that's not important. Now, 'Our Father, Who art in Heaven, thank You for such a wonderful world in which to live. Thank You, too, for our dear friends, for the warm floor, the hot tea and the wonderful surprises. In Jesus's Name, Amen.' "

Wun-yung's Mother peeked out of one eye, not sure whether it was proper yet or not. When she saw the others had opened their eyes, she quickly remarked, "That's nice. I didn't know you could say 'thank you' to Hah-nah-nim so easily. I like it, and I feel good. Is that the way you pray, Outside-Lord?" she asked Kee-haw. "Yes, well not exactly, but pretty much like that," Kee-haw replied.

Wun-sik rose to leave, knowing that he and Kee-haw both needed their rest before another hard day of work. What with humor, banter, wit, repartee, and laughter, the evening had passed very rapidly.

Kee-haw said, "I'll see him to the gate." Turning to Wun-sik, he said, "Go in Peace and always remain in Peace, my good and wonderful friend."

Soon-hee had slipped over during a lull in the conversation and thrown more rice chaff on the coals of the fire in the lean-to of the one room cottage; aside from that brief time, she hadn't missed a word that had been spoken in the sahrahng that evening. She was floating on air as she quietly gathered up the cups and table, put them in the main kitchen and returned again to her little room.

Just to have such a wonderful husband was enough to turn any girl's head. But to think that he could have such a really marvelous friend! Poor man, how very lonely Wun-sik-ssee must be since his wife's death, quite a few months ago. And to think that even with that void in his life, he could be so witty in joshing her Kee-haw, so pleasant and thoughtful toward Wun-yung's Mother, and so winsome when it came to sharing his Faith! Why, wonder of wonders, Wun-yung's Mother had never been so cordial, or so open to the God-light, as she was this evening!

As she walked quickly across the dark courtyard, she couldn't help but wonder rather pensively, "How does my husband feel about the change in this woman he used to call Sourface? And about his best friend, who in one evening, and a short one at that, accomplished more than he could do in eleven years?"

Kee-haw had already gone in and started to undress. "Come in, Paw-bae-yah, my Pearl of Great Price," he greeted her. "Did you know that Jesus talked about you once?" he asked, and a very happy smile suffused his whole face.

"No, tell me about it, wonderful man. How do you know so much?"

"Oh, I really don't, but perhaps it's because I'm so hungry to learn more and keep reading the Book, sweet Paw-bae."

"What book, sweet husband?"

"There is only one Book, Darling, and thank God, you know which one that is," Kee-haw rejoiced. "But don't you recall that story about the man who sold everything that he had so that he could buy that one marvelous Pearl of Great Price? That's you, Paw-bae-yah! Ah-ee-gaw!* I could say a lot of other things about losing such a gem, and feel sorry for you and for myself. But let's not spoil this wonderful evening with anything glum or sour."

"Yes, my Love," she agreed with his negative sentiment in true orinetal fashion. "Isn't it amazing, if not somewhat bewildering, when you stop to think of what God has done for us? Do you suppose that there is some way that we could reciprocate and really let God know how much we love Him for His goodness?"

"Let's think about that, Sweetie. There's something awfully big and tremendous about it. I really don't even like to talk about it, especially this evening. But do you suppose that what we are planning for our lives has some of that in it?"

"Oh! You are so Precious, my Love. How did you think of that? Maybe that will take off some of that sharp, raw edge, so it won't be quite as impossible as we think," Soon-hee agreed, "but as you say, let's change the subject. You just said this was a wonderful evening. Can you explain what you meant?"

"Well, first, I never saw good old Wun-sig-ee in as high form as he was in tonight. Wasn't he superb? He even got through to Wun-yung's Mother. If I hadn't seen it with my own eyes, and heard it with my own ears, I would never have believed it. Of course, God had a hand, too, but Wun-sig-ee was really tops," Kee-haw averred.

"And then, the miracle of miracles, grouchy Sour-face didn't complain once this evening! Whatever has gotten into her! Why the whole atmosphere was simply out of this world! I'm just going to have to figure out a new name for her! Would you help me, Soon-hee? I've used up all the good names I can think of on you!"

Soon-hee politely brushed his compliment aside, saying "Why do you talk like that?" But, nonetheless, Kee-haw could see that she was amused and highly elated, too. Somewhat as an afterthought, she added, "Well, I guess you answered my question all right; thanks a lot. I was thinking almost the same thing as I came across the courtyard. Oh, husband, our very thinking is so similar so many times. But excuse me; maybe I shouldn't have said that! It just makes everything harder, doesn't it? Please forgive me. I wasn't thinking about what I was saying."

A week or so after this episode, Kee-haw found that his mattock, with which he did most of the hard garden cultivation, was so worn down and blunt that it had become an ineffective tool. He decided to take it across town to the blacksmith and have him repair it. Calling and telling the two women of his errand, he paused a moment to be sure he had enough money in his pouch. Then he picked up a piece of scrap-metal he'd been saving quite awhile and with his worn-out gwaeng-ee started out. Fortunately, the blacksmith was caught up with his work, and could start right in on Kee-haw's gwaeng-ee.

"It'll take me at least an hour to do a good job, Paek Older-brother*," he said. "If you have any other errands you'd like to do, go ahead. You know me; I'll do just as good a job, whether you're here or not, and you won't be wasting your time."

Kee-haw rejoined, "I know you're an honest man, Seung-mawg-ee. If you weren't, we'd have run you out of town long ago. How's the family? Everybody well? That's a very good idea of yours; one hates to waste his time. I'll go see if my friend, Wun-sig-ee, is home for lunch already. You know, if he is, he might even ask me to have pot-luck with him. Hey, you should get a bonus for that one. 'Bye."

On his way over to Naw Wun-sik's, Kee-haw passed the time of day with Kim Miller, who had been delivering some freshly ground flour to a housewife and was on his way back to the mill. Kee-haw told him that Soon-hee was all he had said she was and more, that he had never been disappointed in her. He said, "Of course, there are a few problems, as there are in any triangle, but they are never Soon-hee's fault. Please give my regards to your good wife, Kim Miller," he concluded and went on his way.

In less than ten minutes he was at Wun-sik's home. Wun-sik himself had just turned the corner of the lane coming towards him and Kee-haw waited while his friend opened the Great-Gate. "I really should have taken a lunch with me out to the field today," Wun-sik observed, "But I got up late, so I figured it wouldn't take too much longer and maybe even be better for my tummy, if I came home and warmed up something. After all, it's not much over five minutes out to my fields, Kee-haw-yah. What brings you here today? Of course, you know whatever it is, you're always welcome," Wun-sik added as he fumbled with the big padlock.

"Without a woman, I haven't much that's fit to eat around here, Kee-haw-yah. However, if you don't mind a bachelor's pot-luck, join me in a bite of lunch," Wun-sik continued. "It was so much fun when I dropped in a week ago Sunday. I certainly had a very good time and your First-Wife was congenial. You know, I thought for a moment that she was going to tell us that she had decided to become a Christian. After all, God is a wonder-working God. Just look what He's doing with us! Nothing is impossible with Him. Isn't that what you told me, Kee-haw-yah?"

"Sure, I told you that. But haven't you found out yet, Wun-sig-ee, that it's not always easy to apply every religious truth to yourself or your family? And many times it's so easy to excuse yourself," Kee-haw answered.

Wun-sik had left some water in the kettle where he'd cooked his breakfast. The hot coals in the fire underneath had not all gone out, so he added some fuel, and before long the water was steaming. He then added some cold, cooked rice from another covered container, and in very little time, they each sat down to a bowl of hot gruel on which they sprinkled some crushed seaweed and some seasame seed. Both bowed their heads, and Wun-sik, as the Lord-man*, said grace.

Each had a flat, brass spoon with which he noisily consumed the gruel. The sucking action drew cool air across the gruel, so that it could be swallowed sooner without scalding their throats. This saved time.

Kee-haw opened the conversation: "Wun-sig-ee, gradually, I'm getting my unwitting sins straightened out. Poor Soon-hee, she has taken the brunt of everything. She has finally come to the place where she realizes that for the greatest good of all concerned, she must leave me and become the First-Wife of another man. Of course, he would have to be a single man and a good Christian as well. It gets somewhat complicated when you have to figure that he must be someone that she can respect and admire and love.

"We are such good friends, Wun-sig-ee, we have never hidden our innermost thoughts from each other, have we? Of course, neither Soon-hee nor I like this idea one bit. It's just that it seems to be the only way to straighten out our messy family situation. And she hasn't said one word about whether she has thought of someone who might be suitable, and pretty much meets the requirements.

"I'm trying to help by keeping my eyes open. But you can see my predicament, because neither of us likes to talk to the other about it, for fear of causing hurt. And that's the last thing we would want to do. Anyway, you visit markets that I don't go to and see folks whom I don't see. How about your helping us in this search? We'd sure appreciate it, if you don't mind," Kee-haw concluded.

"Well, Kee-haw, I was the one who made the arrangements for you to marry Soon-hee-ssee in the first place. Maybe it is proper that I should unravel my own handiwork. I'll be frank with you as always. As you know, my wife died last winter, a year ago, when food was scarce and disease was not. This single-life is pretty lonely, as you can imagine. Remember, I told you year before last that in my own fanciful, dreamy moments, I too had thought of Soon-hee-ssee! Maybe before I look around too much, I should look inside my own heart and mind and see if the answer to this entanglement isn't right there. But give me some time, Kee-haw-yah, and don't say a word to Soon-hee-ssee yet,'' Wun-sik answered.

Then he continued: "I'm quite new in matters related to this Christian religion, as you well know. It would help me a great deal in my looking inside, if, without divulging any confidences, you could tune me in a little on Soon-hee-ssee's spiritual growth, my friend. At least, I am now aware that growth is the most important thing in anyone's life. Even a small glimpse would help, I'm sure."

Kee-haw was very fond of his life-long friend and felt he was definitely the finest man that he would ever know. Somehow, however, being so close to him, and knowing him as a man, married practically all of his adult life, Kee-haw had failed to think of him as a possible candidate for Soon-hee's hand.

Now that Wun-sig-ee had announced that he might be interested, Kee-haw was highly elated. "You can depend on me, Wun-sig-ee; I won't breathe a word to anyone, least of all to Soon-hee, bless her heart. Women are something very special, don't you think, and some of their ways are quite different from ours. Their feelings are so delicate, and we men are often so rough. Oh! oh! I'm so happy, Wun-sig-ee." He reached around the little table and whacked Wun-sik's knee.

"Of course, you have been aware that Soon-hee has been going with me to the Bible Class and the Worship Service in the Eup Church. That's been almost every Sunday for the last three months. Then again, I believe it was Soon-hee's influence, more than mine, that got my maht-chah-sik*, Wun-sig-ee, going with us each Sunday.

"As you well know, First-Wife has never made things easy for Soon-hee, even though Soon-hee works her head off. That used to get her down badly, so much so, in fact, that many nights she would practically cry herself to sleep. But her newfound Faith has meant so much to her that she hasn't done that for months now. That's about all I can think of right now that isn't confidential, Wun-sig-ee," Kee-haw related.

"Oh, thank you, good friend. You don't know how much that helps me! Give me a few days now to mull these things over. Yesterday was kind of dark and cloudy, but today the atmosphere has changed completely," Wun-sik rejoined. "Can't you get some more of your tools to wear out quickly? It would be so nice for you to have lunch with me every day!"

"Now you're talking!" Kee-haw swatted Wun-sik's knee again. "Only instead of my coming here, you go to our place; in fact, go tomorrow*. If we take turns there'll be absolutely no hardship on either home. And if you go directly from your fields, it won't take much longer than coming here. Then you can see what a good cook she is, too, and probably learn a little more about how sweet and thoughtful she is. These things are important, Wun-sig-ee. Oh, how smart you are to suggest this! Now we're getting somewhere! Why didn't we think of this sooner? I'll just tell her and First-Wife it's to pay you back for today's lunch. Hah! Aren't we the schemers! Remain in peace. See you tomorrow."

Swinging around again past Seung-mawg-ee's, Kee-haw thanked him for his good work, paid him, put his mattock over his shoulder and headed for home. He was positive there were some sort of wings attached to his straw-shoes. "Isn't God wonderful?" he said, almost out loud, sure of the outcome. As long as he had to give up his sweetheart, which, of course, was something at which his whole being rebelled, he might as well appreciate and enjoy the different ways in which the good God softened the blows both for him and her.

"Something Soon-hee said last week, after Wun-sik dropped by for a visit, makes me wonder if Soon-hee isn't beginning to see something in Wun-sig-ee, too," he thought to himself. "Wouldn't that be ideal, if both of them fell in love with each other? At any rate, if I have to lose her, I couldn't lose her to a better man, thank God! I just pray God that I may never be jealous of him!"

He turned the last corner of the homeward lane, the one where he could see his own Great-Gate. Now he heard faithful Blackie giving that high-pitched yelp of "Welcome, Master." Home was home, with all its troubles and frustrations. He'd lost some precious time from his work, but thank God, he'd gained some important things, too!

It was a nice, late-spring afternoon. The two women had gotten tired of waiting for him. They had their lunch tables out on the porch, and with Number Four, were relaxing. They both jumped up and started for the kitchen to get his lunch. He called across and told them he'd already eaten at Wunsig-ee's. "But," he said, "you can't win, because I had to invite him to come and eat with us tomorrow noon. I really feel sorry for him; he's leading a lonely life. Well, I can't rest any this noon. I've lost so much time today, I'll go right back to the fields." Kee-haw smiled to himself as he hurried away. "Wait until they find out what I did with that 'lost time!' "

This is the new home of Dr. and Mrs. Woodbridge O. Johnson, M.D., built about 1902. It was next door (south) to the new home of the Rev. and Mrs. James Edward Adams on East Mountain, the hill west of Tae-goo City. Front row from left, Nellie Dick Adams, Edith Parker Johnson and Martha Scott Bruen. Back row from left, James Edward Adams, Woodbridge O. Johnson, possibly Rev. R. H. Sidebotham, and Harry M. Bruen (home next door — north) to the Adams' home.

CHAPTER XI
A New Chapel

"Come right in, Wun-sig-ee. Since you had to come straight from your fields, I've poured some warm water in this basin so you can wash your hands. Don't hurry; the women-folk haven't got lunch served up yet." Kee-haw was very excited about this new development. He had been turning it over in his mind yesterday afternoon, yesterday evening, and again this morning. He was afraid he would say the wrong thing and spoil everything. Consequently, he just kept quiet until Wun-sik had finished washing.

"It's so nice today, we're just going to eat our lunch on the porch," Kee-haw said. Both women came forward, each with a heavily laden table in her hands. They placed them on the edge of the porch. They slipped out of their shoes, stepped up on the porch, picked up the tables and carried them over to the seated men. Both men bowed their heads in silent prayer, then started eating.

The women had not had time to return down to the kitchen, when Wun-sik remembered his manners. He paused in his eating and said: "I thought Kee-haw invited me to come to lunch! This is the first time in my life that I ever heard a meal with this many dishes called lunch. The big Chosen Hotel in Seoul is advertising for two more cooks. Do you want me to send in your applications? They say they pay well. Before long, you'd all be poo-jah*."

"Sure," First-Wife retorted, "send them a telegram 'going* on tonight's express.' " All four had a hearty laugh and the women disappeared into the kitchen.

Wun-sik and Kee-haw ate their lunch in comparative silence, as is the custom in this Land of the Morning Calm. This, of course, did not surprise the women. They stood around in the kitchen doing things that made the least noise, in hopes that something interesting or gossipy might be said and overheard.

An electrified animation had come across Wun-sik's face as, out of the corner of his eye, he had watched graceful Soon-hee. She had brought Kee-haw's table up onto the porch and over to him. In a way, Wun-sik was grateful that she hadn't brought his own to him. This way, she was pretty close, without occupying the whole horizon.

Wun-sik noticed, however, that the thrill of her temporary nearness had worn off somewhat toward the end of the meal, as it naturally would. So he didn't let this bother him too much. After all, he must be practical. Even if he did marry her, he couldn't be near her all the time!

Down in the kitchen, after a whispered consultation, the two women brought up the after-meal bowls of warm rice-water from the almost empty rice-cauldron. This time, Soon-hee brought Wun-sik's bowl to him. At least, she politely kneeled and placed it on the table in front of him. She was so close that he could have reached out and touched her face or her hands!

Of course, anything even faintly like this was utterly taboo. But the thought was a powerful one. And the aroma of her body was so potent that the deep thrill was far more overwhelming than at first. Soon-hee carefully avoided any eye contact and again unhurriedly retired to the kitchen. Both men made fitting remarks about the flavorful dishes, to which First-Wife made proper replies. She lingered a little, but as the men seemed to be in no hurry to finish their drinks, she too withdrew.

The magic moment was past, but the exhilaration remained in full force. Without a word, Wun-sik, in the complete bliss of High Heaven sipped his warm rice-water. Kee-haw very thoughtfully remained silent, too. Not a sound came from the two women in the kitchen. All that could be heard was the noisy drinking of the water. Then the two men rose and looked very solemnly at each other. Still without another word, they donned their work-straw-shoes, and each went to his own fields.

After the Wednesday evening meeting that week, Wun-sik asked Kee-haw if he could stay for a few minutes. He said, "I want to talk about something I think is very important and vital to our village and the cause of Christ in our village." Then he added, "I don't think it'll take very long."

Kee-haw answered: "Take as long as you please, my friend. Is there anything more important than the cause of Christ here or anywhere?"

Encouraged by this, Wun-sik continued, "Kee-haw-yah, you're the leader of our little group of Christians here in Moojee-moo. You are a man with a family and many responsibilities and not much time for mulling things over. I live alone and have a lot of time in the evenings while I'm resting to do some thinking and planning. The following thought came to me the other evening, but because our Christian group is so closely involved, I wanted to get your opinion first of all.

"As you well know, Kee-haw-yah, many other small villages in our country have tiny groups of Christians and near-Christians or inquirers. One of the first things they do as a group, when there are enough of them, is to build a chapel.

"I have been noticing that very few of our group are attending the regular Sunday Service in the Eup. But keeping the Lord's Day holy, and attending Services regularly are such important parts of our Faith. The study of God's Word and the participation in Holy Communion are important too. You and members of your family attend regularly, I know, but if the rest of us are not benefiting as are you and yours, our progress as a body of Christians is going to be woefully slow.

"What I am trying to say, Kee-haw-yah, is simply this: The Eup-church is too far away for most of us to attend regularly. I think that our greatest need now is to build a chapel. It doesn't need to be big. Two or three kahn* will be ample for quite awhile. A curtain down the middle will take care of separating the sexes. After we get strong enough, and our numbers warrant it, we can build another wing, so as to make the Korean letter 'n' or nah*. Where the two wings join, we can have the pulpit and the women can sit in one wing and the men in the other. But that of course will come later."

Kee-haw broke in at this point, "Wun-sig-ee, where did you ever hear of such a peculiarly shaped building, let alone a Church?"

"Hadn't you heard?" Wun-sik came back. "They are building a great many of them like that up in the northern part of our country, even large Churches, too. Since most of our Churches have more women than men, we could build the smaller men's wing first.

"But to continue with my idea, the men in the five or six homes that have members coming to our meetings should agree on a day. Then we could go high up on the mountain and cut enough trees for the rafters, ridgepole, and upright posts and door and window frames. I have enough extra boards around to make two doors, one on each side at the back. Someone else will doubtless have enough for one more door at the front. Others could donate paper for the windows. If the six families couldn't spare enough straw for the roof, I'm sure our neighbors would all be glad to help a little. If we'd set a day for building it far enough ahead, some of the them might even lend a hand, particularly if we had free lunches that day. Briefly, that's about as far as I've gotten, but I wanted to check with you before going any further. What do you say?"

"I say that you are God-inspired, Wun-sig-ee. The days are getting shorter, and the sooner we get started working on the chapel, the more light we'll have in the evenings, after we return from our farm work, to do the building," Kee-haw answered. "Let's decide first on the day for the mountain trip. The women and younger folks can stay here in the village and get sickles and peel off the bark so the wood will season more quickly."

A few weeks elapsed after the two men's conversation. The agreed upon date had arrived and several men were busy on the mountain, cutting rafter-sized trees.

Kee-haw called out, "We've already cut enough trees to make several chee-ge* loads to go down the mountain. I know it's lots of fun working up here in the rocks and trees. I also know that carrying heavy loads down these rough paths is tricky business. But, several of the more sure-footed of us had better get going."

Kee-haw went on, "I've got my chee-ge ready to go. It won't take too long to load up the cow*, if one of you will help me. Then several of us can go down together. If anyone has any trouble on the way, we can all help each other. Those who are going, please take your lunches. We'll never make it back here in time to eat with the rest of you."

The older men of the village had held their conclave the evening before, agreeing that a new church would add to the dignity of Moo-jee-moo. One of them owned a small parcel of land covered with wild grass close to the homes. Children often played on it. He offered the land to the Jesus Church if the members would care for it and pay the taxes. This parcel of land was the final destination for the rafters. Several of the women-folk had finished their lunches and were waiting, sickles in hand.

"Oh, we thought you'd never get here. You must have cut a lot before you started bringing them down," Soon-hee laughingly commented.

"How right you are. It was so much fun cutting them, and it was so cool up there, under the big trees. To tell you the truth, we forgot all about bringing them down so you could work on them. Please forgive us," Kee-haw apologized back. "But I'll tell you this, we didn't even stop for lunch. We ate as best we could, even while we were carrying those heavy loads."

"Oh, you are noble souls, and we know you are very tired. We'll help you unload. Then you must rest before climbing back up that steep trail. My! How nice and straight these rafters are," another wife complimented.

Still another added, "The kee-doong* must be adzed and shaped quickly so they can start seasoning. Who's the best adzer in the village? Maybe if we ask him, he'll help us. Let's be extra nice to him, so we'll have the best job possible."

Thus they laughed and joked and worked away with a will. More loads kept coming and the men who had brought down the first loads went back for more.

In another two weeks they had the main framework up and were ready to add the rafters. This went quite rapidly. Next came the wattle to support the thatch. Here they used the smaller branches, so it went slowly. Evening after evening, the six men and their wives and the older children worked while the smaller children romped in the grass nearby. In slack moments while waiting below, some of the women started weaving the straw into the big rolls that would facilitate the roll-laying of the thatch. Each of the six families had brought its left-over straw from the previous fall's rice harvest.

Some of the non-Christians came out to watch and offer advice. They rather enjoyed their ring side seats at the building show, since there was no organized entertainment in the village. There wasn't even any possible meeting place, with the exception of the one little room at the Inn. So this was more social life and fun than they'd had for many a moon*. No chairs were needed! If there was no clean place to sit comfortably, cross-legged, anyone could simply squat and enjoy the show for as long as he or she wanted to.

One or two of these self-appointed kibitzers made some fertile suggestions, to the effect that one of these days they might get interested and decide they wanted to be Christians and attend services. It would have been embarrassing if they hadn't helped in building the meeting-house. Following through on their comments, on the following evening, several of them brought their own hammers and saws. Of course, they were gladly and warmly welcomed.

The wattle and daub of the walls came next, while men with more carpentering skills made the three doors. Even before the doors were finished, they had set the date for the first meeting. Kee-haw had seen Ahn Pastor on one market-trip, had kindly offered to come and conduct the church dedication ceremony.

It didn't take long to finish the walls and lay the thatch. Before the doors were hung, Wun-yung volunteered to run around the village with an invitation, written by his father, inviting everyone to the first meeting.

Fortunately, it was not the time of year when the heavy straw-mats* were in use at home. So Kee-haw and Wun-sik went around and borrowed all the mats they needed to cover the hard-packed earth-floor. This would do for a few months until they could afford to install a better floor.

Not realizing that Ahn had already offered to come, one of the early kibitzers suggested that more people would come to their first Chapel Meeting if the Western Teacher were there, especially since he had led the first meeting in Kee-haw's mah-dahng.

It was only a little past the middle of the summer, and they wouldn't need to worry about heating their nice, new chapel for awhile. The three-kahn building would doubtless be packed for the first Service. Of course, they would plan to have a special Feast of Celebration after the meeting.

Another week passed and another Sunday arrived. Wun-sik had decided that Wednesday night studies with Kee-haw and the other new inquirers were fine, but he wanted to be a Christian besides being a man worthy of Soon-hee. So he must quicken the tempo of his progress by going to the Bible Class and Church on Sundays in the Eup.

Wun-sik got up quite a bit earlier than usual to get all his chores done before leaving. Since this was his first time at the Church, he decided to leave earlier than he normally would. He knew that members of the Paek family who attended the Sunday Service in the Eup would probably leave a bit later. Since it was not market-day, the early start would probably give him time to do some much-needed thinking, and this was what he craved.

Five lee or so down the Maw-see-paht road, Wun-sik suddenly stopped short. No one was within earshot, so he started talking to himself, "Soon-hee could very well be pregnant! No one has said anything, but look how long they've been married. And if she is, it's Kee-haw's child. Do I want another man's child running around my house? This is serious business! I'm going to have to have a talk with Kee-haw, which brings me up to the primary question, 'Do I love her? Do I really want her to be my wife? Will she be a good mother to the children that God is probably going to bless us with?'

"If the answer is unequivocally 'yes' to all three, then I can put up with the other things that I would rather not have. All of which really means, 'How much do I love her? How much do I really want her to be my wife?' I remember Kee-haw once mentioning that she is very sweet and capable with his other children. That's probably the answer to my third question, so that there are only two remaining."

During the course of this conversation with himself, he had resumed his walking, making some effort to make up for the time he'd lost.

Occasionally, Wun-sik looked back to see if the Paeks were in sight. But the road twisted, and he didn't see them before he reached the church.

On his trips to market in the Eup, Wun-sik had inquired where Ahn Pastor, the missionary, lived. He had been told he lived up on the hill at the west end of town, the hill called East Mountain*. He had met Ahn at the evening meeting at Moo-jee-moo, so it wasn't like looking up a complete stranger. Somehow, he felt that talking with Ahn would help. Arriving early, he went past the church to Ahn's home.

When he got fairly close to the house, he stopped a well-dressed stranger who looked intelligent and asked him about the path to the missionary's home. The stranger replied, "Go through the second Great-Gate on your left. Go straight up the lane, and at the top, the only door you will see in his house, besides the cellar door, is the one to the men's parlor. Just hit it three times with your fist. He has probably finished his morning meal by now."

Wun-sik thanked the stranger and followed his instructions. He found that the lane went up the hill between two thick hedges of trifoliate orange thorn-bushes, with fruit resembling a light-colored lime.

A friend of Wun-sik's who lived in the Eup had told him how Ahn had agreed to build the missionary residences west of the crest of the hill in order to avoid blocking the flow of heavenly blessings that came down the east side of the hill into the city. Only thus could he get permission from the Governor of the Province to build Western homes on East Mountain.

Wun-sik was fortunate. Ahn Pastor himself opened the door. "It's been a long time since I last saw you, Naw Teacher," Ahn greeted him. "How have you been?"

"Yes, it's been a long time all right. We wish you could visit Moo-jee-moo oftener, Ahn Pastor," Wun-sik answered. "I've been pretty well, thank you."

"I hear you have been regular in your attendance at the Wednesday evening study group. That makes me very happy. But please have a seat over here, where the light from the windows won't be in your eyes, Wun-sik-ssee," Ahn returned. "This is not a market-day. Is there something special that has brought you to the city so early?"

"Yes, Ahn Pastor, I was hoping that you would have some time for us to talk over something," Wun-sik replied. "It's been bothering me."

"You must have walked in from Moo-jee-moo quickly this morning to get here this early. Since you are early, there's quite a bit of time. Then, of course, we can continue our conversation on the way down to the Bible Class. That is, I'm presuming that you don't want to miss it. Please tell me what's on your mind," Ahn encouraged.

"You know, Ahn Mawk-sah, it's so easy to talk to you. I believe you care about us Koreans and our problems."

"Of course. This is a foreign land to me, Wun-sik-ssee. I wouldn't be here if I didn't care. Now, can you tell me?" Ahn asked again.

"Well, it's like this, Honorable Mawk-sah. This winter that's past left me a single man again, as you perhaps have heard. It has been a lonely time, of course. I mention this, not because I crave sympathy, but only that you may understand the ramifications a little better. Let me go back a few years. I might mention that in the hidden privacy of my adolescence, I sometimes imagined that I was in love with Kim Soon-hee. Even after my parentally-arranged marriage, if I had time for daydreams, I toyed with the idea of Soon-hee-ssee as a second wife, if I accumulated enough wealth.

"I even admitted this to my best friend, Kee-haw, when last year I offered to be the go-between for him and Soon-hee-ssee. Now these two, in accordance with God's Word and Will, have come to a parting of the ways. I have been doing a little reminiscing. I am just a beginner in the things of this Jesus Doctrine. And I am wondering if perhaps I might be the one, under God's hand, of course, who might be the proper mate for Soon-hee-ssee.

"I might add that she appeals to me very strongly, though at the same time, I realize that this may be more physical than mental and spiritual. What do you think, Honorable Mawk-sah? I come to ask you because I know that you have studied God's Word more than any of us," Wun-sik concluded.

"Wun-sik-ssee, it is my loss that I haven't gotten to know you better sooner. Not long ago, Kee-haw-ssee told me that you were coming to the Wednesday-night class at his house. I presume that in this and other ways you have had opportunities to see Soon-hee-ssee. And you have witnessed little things, such as her care of Kee-haw-ssee's children, and her attitude toward First-Wife. These will help you evaluate her personality in relation to yours.

"I know, myself, that she has a very kind and loving disposition. She has also been a great asset to Kee-haw-ssee in helping him get through an almost impossible period in his life, however, I am well aware that these traits and qualities do not necessarily mean that you two would be compatible. You are doing very well to get advice from different perspectives, but in the end, Wun-sik-ssee, you, under God, must make the final decision. She is of course, considerably younger than you. But she is much more mature than many other unmarried girls in Moo-jee-moo, don't you think?'' Ahn offered.

"That's true," Wun-sik responded, "but then Moo-jee-moo is not the only place that I can look for a wife. I'll be very honest with you, Honorable Mawk-sah. I have a peculiar feeling that I could look a long, long time and many, many places, and still not find anyone else that would measure up to Soon-hee!

"There's one thing particularly that I'd like to get your opinion on, Honorable Mawk-sah. Just a few days ago, it suddenly occurred to me that Soon-hee-ssee could very well be pregnant. Even this morning, the idea hit me again with renewed force. Some people don't talk about such matters until it becomes obvious, and even then not too much. I have wondered if having Kee-haw's child running around our house might not be a cause for friction. It might even make for an unhappy marriage."

"I would think, Wun-sik-ssee, that that would depend largely on you and your love for Soon-hee-ssee. The child would be born under your roof, and raised within your care and tutelage. It seems to me that you, with your newfound Christian approach to everything, could love such a child very much. Possibly more than your very own, that is, if you are truly Christian.

"After all, the child would be your own wife's child and the child of your best friend. Under the circumstances, there isn't much more you could ask, is there?" Ahn asked.

"Now that you put it that way, it sounds pretty good, Ahn Mawk-sah. In fact, it rather reinforces some ideas that have been floating around in my head this morning," Wun-sik said.

"Isn't that strange? You just finished saying, 'It depends largely on your love for Soon-hee-ssee.' That's exactly what I figured out myself on my early hike this very morning. If my love for her is great enough, I'll be willing to put up with some things that otherwise I would rather not have. And, of course, it won't be the child's fault that I am not the father! Which leads me to another problem . . .

"At present we are only guessing. But if and when there is such a child, he or she will not even know that I'm not his or her father. Why even tell the child? Wouldn't it be better if he or she never knew? If Kee-haw's willing, I could even arrange to adopt him or her legally."

"Well, my friend," the missionary answered, "you don't need to settle all your problems before they arrive! Maybe further light will come on some of them as time goes on. But by the time we get to the church, it'll almost be time for the Bible Class to start, so maybe we can continue the conversation as we walk down and over."

As they took the brisk fifteen minute walk, they resumed their conversation, though this time in somewhat subdued tones. They didn't care to share such intimate thoughts with acquaintances and unknown passers-by.

"Actually, Ahn Mawk-sah I want to be worthy to marry such a fine woman as Soon-hee-ssee. So I'd better spend more time learning about the Jesus Way of life. That's the main reason for coming to the Eup this morning. I've never been to a regular Church Service yet, or a regular Bible Class. So today will be unique for me. Our visit this morning was sort of an afterthought bonus, you might say," Wun-sik offered.

Ahn relished his Sunday morning stroll with his new friend. He also appreciated the fact that this man who hardly knew him had come to him for advice and counsel. It was rather an humbling experience, and deep in his heart he prayed that he might measure up to this trust. How could he, who had never intimately encountered a plural-wife situation, know how to advise? The good Lord must put the words right into his heart and mouth.

Ahn decided to be very frank and open, as he replied, "Wun-sik-ssee, you may not realize it, but I'm an American from the other side of the world. And the very idea of simultaneous marriage to two women is a very unique and strange thing. Of course, we know that thousands of years ago, polygamy was allowed because of the hardness of men's hearts. But that was in the days of the Old Testament. And even two thousand years ago, Jesus did not condone it. Tell me, Wun-sik-ssee, in your culture, do you have no ethical feelings or conscience at all about polygamy? You see, this is my first face-to-face encounter with such a situation!"

"To be very truthful, Ahn Mawk-sah," Wun-sik returned, "very few people that I have encountered have ever considered the ethics of such a relation. We usually avoid any such thinking. The common comment is something like this, 'Oh, what a lucky man to be able to afford a second or third wife,' as the case might be. Of course, after we become Christians, it's a different story, but that's because the perspective is also a great deal different."

By this time they were turning in the Great-Gate of the churchyard. The missionary escorted his new friend to the pastor's study. There he introduced him to that remarkable Korean, the Rev. Lee Wun-yung*. Though as blue-blooded as any of the true aristocracy of the country, Lee was nevertheless as devout and humble and as inspiring a person as anyone might meet. It was almost time for the Bible class to begin, so all three kept their remarks very brief.

Wun-sik especially was in a hurry to get over to the sanctuary, hoping to have at least a glimpse of sweet Soon-hee as she came across the courtyard.

CHAPTER XII
Wun-sik's First Sunday School And Church Service And Wun-yung's First Job

Fortunately, Kee-haw had informed Wun-sik about what to expect in his first Sunday School and formal, public Worship Service. It wasn't quite the nightmare that it had been for Kee-haw. Wun-sik soon spotted Kee-haw on the men's side of the curtain, pulled Ahn's sleeve and said, not too softly, "Come on; let's sit near Kee-haw." He waved his hand at him and called across, "We're going over to sit with you."

Ahn touched Wun-sik's arm, shook his head and whispered, "Sh-h-h, we're in God's House. We try to be quiet and reverential."

By the time they had moved over and sat on the floor again, the first hymn had begun. Wun-sik found the place in his hymnal and did his best to give the appearance and the sound of lusty singing. But his mind was on Soon-hee, whom he knew must be somewhere on the other side of that awful curtain, stretched all the way down the middle of the room.

As he bellowed the hymn, with the hymnbook held in front of his eyes at the proper distance, he let his eyes wander sideways, on the side away from Ahn and Kee-haw and toward the curtain.

"Oh," he said to himself, "of course, that's why they have the curtain. How would anyone in love keep his mind on the Worship and toward God, if his sweetheart were in plain sight! Some people still think that Church Services are indecent without a curtain, I suppose. Well, indecent or not, if I could only see through that nuisance of an obstruction! Aren't Koreans slightly old-fashioned? Maybe I can catch a glimpse of her after the meeting, when the mass of women flow like a stream out of the back door on the other side. Then they will go down the step and delta out on the courtyard level."

In lieu of anything to look at, Wun-sik let his mind wander while mouthing the words of the hymn. Soon-hee was pretty, there was no denying it; yet any man's head could be turned by that. He must go deeper. She dressed neatly and freshly and simply, all of which was in her favor! It appealed to him. He certainly didn't like a dirty, bedraggled woman, always wiping her hands on her already filthy apron!

"And then her hair! That would always be a woman's glory. And hers, particularly, is so soft and smooth and glossy! It actually shines, even though it is jet-black!"

The more he let his thoughts wander beyond the "forbidding curtain," the more he wanted to let them wander. And the less important seemed to be his first Sunday School.

"Could it be possible," he continued thinking, "that there is something more important in my life than this new faith and the vast implications of the Great God of Heaven's LOVE for his children? Could it be that I, Wun-sik, am truly in love with this woman to whom I have hardly said a word? But what about all my problems, my worries?

"Well, maybe these wandering thoughts are to remind me of my morning's goal, which was to prepare myself to be a better husband to whomever I marry," he concluded. He lifted his eyes and breathed a prayer, "Help me, please, to get the most from this Service. Help me to pray and praise and learn."

With the hymn over, he opened his Bible and tried to find the passage that was announced. "Did anyone else ever have trouble with straying thoughts in a Sunday School or Worship Service? Am I the only one? Would a loving God forgive, especially when I am not the least bit sorry, and probably have never enjoyed another five minutes quite so much? Maybe no one else was in love as much as I am! Could the God of Love frown on love? If He is really the God of Love, wouldn't he smile and approve?"

Or was he feeling guilty because he was in Sunday School but thinking of Soon-hee? Again he lifted his inner eyes, "You know I love you, Father, and You know whether or not this thing in my heart is true love for Soon-hee. If it is, I know You approve, though while I am here, help me to pay attention and learn all I can. Amen."

Was every new Christian so slow in finding his or her place in the Bible reading? At that juncture, Ahn Pastor realized Wun-sik's dilemma, reached over and quickly found the place for him. He had missed several of the opening verses, but Ahn helped him catch up with the reader.

As far as Wun-sik could see, every one of the many people around him had long since found the place. They were now engrossed in following the reading. "Maybe I'll get better with more practice! I certainly hope so!"

After the two o'clock Church Service, Kee-haw and Wun-sik walked together all the way home to Moo-jee-moo. Engaged in animated conversation, neither of them seemed to be aware that they were being followed. Only a few feet behind them were two others, Kim Soon-hee, the Second-Wife, and Paek Wun-yung, Kee-haw's firstborn.

There was nothing unusual about this order. Even if Kee-haw and Soon-hee had been going somewhere by themselves, Kee-haw would have walked in front and Soon-hee several paces to the rear. This was simply the proper way for a man and wife to walk together! It might be pointed out that the country cow-trails or paths were not usually wide enough for two people to walk side by side, which accounted for only part of the reason for this ancient custom.

However, it would be far from the truth to say that either of the men was actually unaware of the two behind. Whenever there was even a short lull in the forward-conversation, Wun-sik would strain his ears to catch every word that passed between the two behind. He felt deeply that this was a wonderful, God-given chance to understand this remarkable woman.

For his part, Kee-haw hoped fervently that Wun-sik was making the most of this good opportunity. It was

Wun-sik's golden chance to size-up Soon-hee and figure out whether she would make him a suitable wife.

Once in awhile, when Wun-sik was sure that Soon-hee's attention was centered elsewhere, and when he felt that Kee-haw wasn't too observant, he would steal a glance at Soon-hee. He was trying to determine whether her proportions gave away Kee-haw's and her secret or not. Since he was in front and normally facing the opposite direction, this one hundred and eighty degree maneuver was not the easiest to accomplish! Toward the end of the hour and a half walk, Wun-sik wasn't any more sure of the answer than he was at the outset.

Two or three mah-jahng* from Moo-jee-moo, Wun-sik screwed up his courage and called Wun-yung to come up closer. He was learning so little from his eavesdropping that he was becoming quite impatient. Maybe a conversation would reveal something.

"Look here," he began. "You and I don't know each other very well, do we? Let's talk awhile. You've been going with your father to Sunday School and Church every Sunday for quite a few months, haven't you?"

"Yes, sir, and for the last two months my Little Mother has been coming with us, too. It's a lot more fun now because she knows the names of many things my Honorable Father never even noticed," Wun-yung answered.

"Isn't that nice? Do you like to learn new names and things?"

"Oh, yes, sir. In school, so far, the teachers have never taught us the names of birds and flowers like my Little Mother does. She's so nice to all us kids!" Wun-yung volunteered. "She always takes time to explain things."

"Well, you've been to Sunday School and Church so much more than I have. Perhaps I ought to hire you as my teacher to help me catch up," Wun-sik laughingly joked with the boy. "What are your fees?"

"If you please, sir, you are exaggerating a thousand times ten thousand*. But since you and my Honorable Father are such good friends, perhaps he would let me go over for an hour or two Saturday afternoon. I could go by on the way home from school and help you with the farm work or whatever. Then we could talk a little, too," Wun-yung offered.

"You know, that sounds nice. There are lots of things around the place where some help would come in handy. If your father agrees, let's just plan on your coming next Saturday. And be sure and tell your Honorable Mother not to expect you home for lunch," Wun-sik concluded. "How about it, Kee-haw-yah?"

"Maybe he can get some of his Saturday chores done early Saturday before he goes to school. And if he only works for you an hour or two, early in the afternoon, he'll have time after he gets home for the rest of the chores and his Monday-homework," Kee-haw returned. "And anyway, Wun-sig-ee, please don't give him the big-head, calling him a teacher. There are times when he thinks he knows more than I do right now!" Then he turned to Wun-yung, "All right, son; you may go back to your Little Mother, as you call her. It's crowded with all three of us up here in front."

They were much closer to their home-village now. Familiar noises were impinging, and they were beginning to recognize friends and acquaintances. Kee-haw was passing some of his own fields. One of the neighbors, Hawng In-sahng, who was working in a nearby field, called over to him. "Wish I were a poo-jah* and could take the day off whenever I felt like it. What do you do, work nights to make up for the weekly holiday?"

To which Kee-haw quickly answered, "I know you're just jealous. I'll bet you have more in your choo-mu-nee* right now than I have in mine. Come on and show me, or take back what you said!" Then as an afterthought he added, "No, In-sahng-ee, since you are one of my best friends, I'll tell you the truth. That's exactly what I **used** to say about all the Jesus-believing-People."

Thus was Kee-haw learning, by the grace of God, to take affronts and near insults. In a well-poised, hearty way, he would turn them into friendly encouragement to inquire further about the Faith.

Almost a week had passed. Saturday arrived. Wun-yung wrapped up his old, nearly-worn-out trousers in a clean rag which he tied with a scrap of straw-rope he'd saved from somewhere. He headed off for his half-day of school. Today was a big day in his life, the first day he'd ever worked for someone else, that is, someone outside the family.

True, he wasn't being paid in cold cash, but a good, warm meal was nothing to be ignored in these days of high prices. No one could really blame him for having a somewhat warm, proud feeling somewhere under his well-padded ribs.

Back at home, a family conference of two adults was in progress. First-Wife had worked herself up into quite a dither. "Wun-yung is almost as strong as I am. Then on the one day of the week that he has extra time to do extra work around here besides his regular chores, he takes off! To do what? To earn some much needed money? No! Of course not! Just to have a good time! To help someone! How wonderful! Free labor for whoever thinks he needs it! Big stuff, I must say!"

Kee-haw was somewhat amused. But under his surface-affability one could see that he resented this questioning of his right to let Wun-yung help his friend Wun-sik for an hour or two. "Look, Wun-yung's Mother; it's only for a couple of hours at the most, and he'll gain some good experience. You see, he'll be working for someone else for a change. We can't keep him tied up to our home forever, you know."

"Oh, we can't, huh? Have you gone quite insane? You know as well as I do that the ancient custom of our whole nation is for the sons to bring their wives to the parents' homes. How else would the mother have help with the household chores in her old age?" Wun-yung's Mother returned.

"I know all the little things around the house that you never seem to have time to do. Wun-yung's getting big enough and old enough to do at least some of them."

"You are perfectly right, Wun-yung's Mother. I agree with you. I told him to be home by half-past three at the latest. From then on until dark, you'll have him almost four full hours, when he can do nothing but what you assign him. And if you save the inside jobs until the last, he might be able to put in another half hour or so and still have time to finish all his school homework for Monday before bedtime," Kee-haw rejoined. "Now, if you don't mind, I have a few things myself that I'd like to get done today. I'm not getting them done as long as we stand here arguing."

And with that Kee-haw stepped into his old, straw workshoes and stalked around to the other side of the house.

In the meantime, Wun-yung had arrived at Wun-sik's home. "Well, Wun-yung-ee, I'm so glad to see you. You know, Sunday when I got home and all during the week, I've been wondering if your own mother was going to allow you to come and work for me today," Wun-sik greeted his young friend. "She probably has things she saves for you to do on Saturday afternoon."

"No, as far as I know, she didn't make any trouble, but I didn't even ask her permission. Maybe I should have. I was pretty sure from our Sunday afternoon conversation that I had Father's, and I guess I thought that was enough," Wun-yung answered. "Now, what would you like me to do?"

"Well, I'm certainly not going to work you on an empty stomach, and you didn't bring a lunch, did you?" Wun-sik questioned. One could see that Wun-yung was slightly embarrassed. He shook his head negatively and Wun-sik went on, "No, I wouldn't even treat a plow-cow that way. Now come up on the porch."

Their lunch consisted of leftover soup, which Wun-sik had heated, and some cold rice. It was very commonplace, but Wun-yung ate heartily with teenage exuberance. He dipped a spoonful of rice at a time into the hot soup, thus tempering the soup and warming the rice.

"Naw Teacher, your soup is delicious and so healthful, with rice added," Wun-yung complimented very nicely, considering his twelve short years.

Wun-yung worked hard for his age and finished the work Wun-sik asked him to do even before three o'clock. He bade Wun-sik goodbye and ran most of the way home.

Wun-sik announced, "I've come back, everyone," as he stepped over the high sill of the Great-Gate. Following an old oriental custom, the younger children looked up from their play and welcomed him. As he approached the kitchen, the two women looked up from their work. Soon-hee smiled, raised her hand and said, "Hi, hard-working man!"

His mother looked first at the clock on the shelf and said, "Oh, it's only a few minutes after three. Thanks for coming home a little early. Your father thought you might not get here till half-past three. You know there are many things on which I need your help."

Wun-yung replied: "Oh, I'm sorry, Honorable Mother. Strangely enough, I was just telling Naw Teacher awhile ago that I should have checked with you to be sure you could spare me that long. Please forgive me, Honorable Mother; I'll try not to ever do that again."

"Well son, at least tell me about your first job away from home. Did he pay you anything?" his mother asked. "And tell me, was it Naw Teacher who thought to send you home early?"

"The answer is 'Yes' to both questions, Honorable Mother. He was so nice. He said I worked so hard, a hired man couldn't have done any better. And he said I earned my lunch several times over. And he also said, 'Shoes and clothes are getting more expensive nowadays. I know you offered to help me as a friendly neighbor, but still I don't want you or your parents to be out anything. Please take this ten-chun* piece back to them.' Imagine, ten chun for just working an hour or two, and lunch besides. Here it is, Honorable Mother. Please take it.'' Wun-yung opened his money-pouch and gave his mother the shiny, ten-chun piece.

"He's a very nice man, isn't he?" Wun-yung's Mother returned. "He must be very lonely, but tell me, what in the world did you talk about for a whole hour and a half?"

"You'd be surprised, Honorable Mother, we talked about more things than you could imagine! We even talked about our new Little Mother and the names of the birds and the flowers and even some bugs she has been teaching me on the way to Bible Class, Sunday morning," Wun-yung answered.

"How very interesting, Wun-yung-ee; but if we don't get started on our jobs here, we're not going to get them done. Come along, and I'll show you the first one."

CHAPTER XIII
First-Wife's First Church Service

The sun hung quite low in the sky as a gorgeous Korean sunset cast a rosy glow on everything. Kee-haw came back to the courtyard to see Wun-yung-ee working extra hard in an attempt to make up for the time he'd been gone. Wun-yung's Honorable Mother was as elated as any of the family had ever seen her. She had caught sight of Kee-haw before he got to the Great-Gate and called to him to apprise him of what a big help Wun-yung-ee had been. Kee-haw went straight to the woodpile where the lad was chopping some pine wood to the right size for kitchen use. Very proudly and lovingly he congratulated him. He also added, "Be sure to stop in time to finish your Monday's homework, son." He emphasized the words with a big hug and went to clean up.

Five or six minutes later, First-Wife asked Soon-hee to give the call for dinner. As the evenings were beginning to get chilly, they started to carry the tables up into the living room.

When all had assembled and each was seated at his or her individual table, Kee-haw held up a hand. "You know," he said, "I think that today has been one of the nicest days that our family has ever had. Why don't we all commemorate this, yes, and celebrate it? Let's wait to start in on this wonderful meal for just a moment and offer our gratitude to the God of Heaven. I know tomorrow is His special day, but today has been special, too. Wun-yung's Mother, I'm sure you really know there's a God in Heaven. Would you please excuse the rest of us for this moment?"

"You're right. It's been a pretty nice day for us. If you think that Hah-nah-nim would like us to tell him so, it's fine with me," the matriarch returned.

The day and the food having been blessed, a sudden hush fell upon them as they turned their attention to the meal. They were just too busy eating to take time to talk!

But Kee-haw was doing some deep thinking. He had had intimations a few times before that Wun-yung's Mother was fundamentally not so bad. Perhaps his innate desire for cheerfulness and joy had blinded him to some of her good qualities. Could it possibly be that if he recognized and appreciated these when they made their rare appearances, they might appear oftener? Perhaps this was the secret that he had failed to grasp, and, failing, had caused him to blunder into this **impossible triangle**.

Wun-sig-ee had better make up his mind soon. Or else he, Kee-haw, had better get Ahn Mawk-sah to look around for another husband. Possibly Lee-Mawk-sah would have some good suggestions. Or could it be that the time was not quite ripe? Or maybe Wun-sig-ee needed more time to assemble his convincing array of facts. After all, Wun-sig-ee must satisfy himself, without any pushing from anyone else. Perhaps it would be well if he, Kee-haw, made it plain to Wun-sig-ee that he was accessible and available. That is, just in case there were questions to which he had the answers. Possibly this would help speed up the decision.

But was speed really important? Certainly not, if the results were not good and permanent. Of course, now that he, and to a certain extent, Soon-hee, had made up their minds, they wanted to get it over with quickly. But it was always possible that God in his Heaven had a different time schedule. Yes, true, God's clocks could be different from that of humans. So, "Patience, Kee-haw, patience!" was his admonition to himself.

Soon-hee's mind had not been idle either while she was busy eating. Conversation was typically at a minimum, and it was a good time to do a little thinking. She was truly a fortunate woman! Was there another woman on earth with such a really good man for a husband? First-Wife had been badly upset and angry at Wun-yung's working elsewhere this afternoon. But look how Kee-haw had reasoned with her and mollified that old matriarch. It was simply unbelievable!

Then there were the wonderful times when she, Soon-hee, had him practically all to herself on the trips to and from the church! How sensitive he was, always trying to think of some way that he could help ease any strain or solve any problem that she had! Any love that she had ever known or heard of usually had some selfish angle to it. But look at this man! It was breaking his heart in two and practically killing him. But he was doing his best to find her another man with whom she would be more truly and permanently happy.

On the other hand, would she ever be truly happy with any other man? Why should she even think of letting them look for another, when she had this remarkable Kee-haw right now? Wasn't the search rather ludicrous and pointless? But she'd been over every one of these points before and had practically decided that there was only one good answer, even if she accepted it only reluctantly. Of course, that was providing they could find the right man. She would simply have to be patient! Yes, patience was the word.

Wun-yung's Mother had been just as quiet as the rest. Maybe, she wasn't quite sure, but from small clues she had picked up here and there, she seemed to have concluded that there was a scheme of some sort afoot. Kee-haw was quite sure that she sensed this; but he knew that what she wanted to know most of all was whether she would profit or lose in the end. And then there were the children, too. They must have every opportunity that any others had.

Both Kee-haw and First-Wife had to admit that Wun-yung had been bringing home better grades from school. He had also been much more helpful around the house, since he'd been accompanying his father to that church. In God's wisdom, there was probably some reason for this. Certainly it was not mere coincidence. Sometimes, of course, things just happened, and that was it. But not this.

Kee-haw thought, "Thank God for Soon-hee! For a fact, she really turned out a lot of hard work around the place, and life was a lot easier for Wun-yung's Mother than it used to be. Maybe, after all, First-Wife would find out that smiles and laughter did lighten loads!

"At the same time, she would not want to feel that she was losing her managerial grip. She was delegating so many things to Soon-hee! Quite a few adjustments had been made and rightly so. Maybe more would have to be made before everything ran as smoothly as it should."

By all the powers that be, Kee-haw knew that First-Wife was perfectly able to make them, come what may. If the rest of the family came along with her, fine. If not, there would be trouble! They could be sure of that. Judging by today's results, maybe if each family member were a bit more patient, things would run more smoothly!

The small children had been chattering off and on with each other, but for some time they had been aware that adults didn't enjoy talking during meals, and so they pretty much limited their chatter to themselves. Wun-yung had taken his individual table from the children's group to the far side of the adult group. Evidently he felt that he was really getting to be a young man. Just look at all the work and duties and responsibilities that had devolved upon his broadening shoulders! How quickly he was growing up! The farther he got away from the little rascals, the older and more mature he would feel. Here he was, bringing home money to help the whole family with its expenses, just like any day-laborer! How could the family get on without him? And he was only twelve years old!

Wun-yung mustered up his courage and blurted out, "The most thrilling part of the day was talking with that very nice man, Naw Wun-sik-ssee. He was so friendly and not a bit condescending, even though he knows so much more. That was the nicest talk I ever had with an adult, at least as far as I can remember. And I've never found anyone who was so interested in every member of our family, especially my sweet, new Little Mother!"

Kee-haw, to avoid both suspicion and embarrassment, quickly changed the subject: "Tomorrow's Sunday and several of us will be gone most of the day. I know that you three older children don't mind walking as far as the Eup. Instead of dividing the family, why don't we **all** go and take a picnic lunch

150

with us? I'll carry little Wun-bawg-ee, whenever he gets tired, though Wun-yung-ee, our new wage-earner, is big enough to help some on that.

"What do you say, Wun-yung's Mother? Wouldn't that be fun? It would do you good to take a day off and just enjoy yourself with your children."

Putting his question in this way, Kee-haw had deprived Wun-yung's Mother of the excuse of having to baby-sit Wun-Bawk, the youngest child. Wun-bawk was old enough to understand that he had to be quiet during the church service, so Kee-haw wasn't concerned on that account.

Everyone could see that Wun-yung's Honorable Mother was not answering promptly. It was a real temptation to take a day off. Why, she had never had one in her life! That is, except when she was in labor or ill with some inside sickness. Of course, with everybody gone, it would be even more restful right here at home. So she decided to hold out for this expedient.

"That's a wonderful idea," she said, "but I'll tell you a better one. Soon-hee and I will fix a nice lunch for you, and you go. I'm going to stay at home and have a quiet day by myself. Then I'll have a nice, hot supper ready for you when you get home. How's that suit you?"

"Oh U-mu-nee*, it's been such a wonderful half-hour here, with our family together," Wun-yung fairly broke into the conversation. "I think our Honorable Dad just wants it to go on for a lot longer. Won't you please come? It can't be the same without you!"

"Yes, yes, yes," chimed in the other three children, almost in one breath. "Of course you must come," little Sayt-jjae added. "And my Little Mother and I will get up early and get the breakfast and lunch. You don't need to even bother with that."

"Oh, you sweet kids. I guess I'm pretty lucky to have you. Maybe I should enjoy you more. Well, since you're all lined up against me, I guess I'll have to give in," Wun-yung's Mother burst out. "But it's an awful long walk there and back." Then as an after-thought, "Who's going to carry me when my feet get sore?" She looked around the circle of faces and every single one, including Wun-bawg-ee, was smiling at her joke.

"Oh, U-mu-nee, you are so funny! Tell Daddy to bring his chee-ge*. Then he can carry you when he's not carrying me," little Wun-bawg-ee laughingly suggested.

The following morning, although it was the largest group ever to take the trip to the Eup, they got an early start. The early departure was fortunate, as their pace was not as fast as when the group was limited to adults, or older folk.

They had gone about seven or eight mah-jahng*, or roughly half the distance, when Tool-jjae happened to look back. He saw that Naw Wun-sik, who had been nowhere in sight earlier, had almost caught up with them, bringing the number of their troupe to eight. Paying slight attention to the rest of them, Wun-sik went right up to Wun-yung's Mother. "Did you sleep in peace, Honorable Wun-yung's Mother?" he greeted her with a low bow.

She acknowledged the salutation with a return bow. Putting her hand up to the side of her mouth, so that not too many others would hear, she mumbled, "My feet are getting sore already."

"Oh, pity!" Wun-sik said. "Just wait here in the shade of this willow awhile until I go back and hitch up my ox to the wagon. We've got some old bedding around that will make a good cushion. These men that take better care of their draft animals than they do of their Honorable Wives!" He whanged Kee-haw on the back and started for home. "Why, the least you could have done was to bring your pah-jee-ge*," he threw back over his shoulder.

"Some friend, you are!" Kee-haw returned, "making me the laughingstock of my whole family! I should clobber you for that! Wait till I get you out behind the ox-shed some dark night! So you are going to further insult me by getting **your** wagon, when **mine** is closer! Go ahead, if that's what you've set your mind on, but I'll have mine here first, so there!

And we sure don't need two, even if all the kids and grown-ups ride!"

"Well, you do have a point there," Wun-sik snapped back. "But you're carrying the little fellow. By the time you get yourself turned around and the child untied and down, I'll be halfway home. So you haven't got a chance of beating me, even if my home is farther across town."

At that moment, timid Soon-hee could take it no longer and broke in. "While you two noble men are standing there talking about it, the rest of us could have walked on and gotten to the Bible Class! I have a feeling that both of you just like to talk big! That's what I think! As long as it's action that's going to win this race, why don't you start moving?"

In the end, it was Wun-yung's Mother who helped settle the argument. "Look, both of you! If this isn't all talk, to see who can beat the other with his sharp tongue, just let me say a word. I know that men and boys like races. That's fine. But it's probably nine o'clock by now and getting hotter all the time. If I'm not highly mistaken, we're at least halfway to Maw-see-paht. I'll walk very softly the rest of the way, and then there'll be a long rest before the walk back.

"If my feet get too sore on the way home, and worse comes to worst, you ambitious men could have your wonderful race beginning at this same spot, or somewhere else along the way. The rest of us would keep on walking until you came, so it wouldn't be nearly so long a race. And you two huskies would have a little more vim left to do your work this coming week. How does that sound to you?"

"Since it was my idea in the first place," Wun-sik answered, "let me say that I agree with you wholeheartedly. I certainly wasn't using my good sense. This way we won't miss half of the Bible Class, either."

Even the younger folks agreed. So they all went on, though a trifle more slowly. In about an hour they were inside the church courtyard.

"Well, well, well, what a nice surprise, Wun-yung's Honorable Mother. I'm so very glad you came, with your nice big family. Surely you are tired," Ahn warmly greeted the cavalcade. Let's step over to Lee Mawk-sah's sah-rahng. I'm sure he would like to meet you and the younger children. And don't leave us, Wun-sik-ssee. With eight of you Moo-jee-mooers coming to church here, we'll have to find some way of pushing the walls out to make more room!" Ahn added.

Wun-yung's Mother reached out her hand to lean very heavily on Ahn Pastor's arm. "Yes, but right now, Honorable Mawk-sah, I'm more interested in resting for several hours. Let someone else push the walls out. If we don't find some place soon, I'm going to have to sit down in the middle of this churchyard. Please, someone, quickly! I've got to get off my feet before they kill me!"

Kee-haw stepped up speedily and took one arm. Wun-sik took the other. "Come this way," Kee-haw said. "Lee Mawk-sah's study is over here. Please forgive me for being so slow and inattentive. You did marvelously to come so far without having to rest any more than you did. I've always said, 'Slow and steady does it,' and here we are."

Lee Mawk-sah had heard the unexpected commotion in his courtyard. He had thrown open the door, with a "Well, who do we have here? Several folks I've never seen before! We should introd . . . ."

But this time, Kee-haw interrupted the introductory remarks that would take more precious time, by going up to Lee and explaining the emergency. Lee reacted quickly, stepping down to the courtyard level, and taking Wun-yung's Mother's hands. Together, he, Kee-haw and Wun-sik helped her up onto the stoop. With her cooperation, they turned her around and seated her on the small porch while Kee-haw and Lee slipped off her shoes, with apologies on Lee Pastor's part. In normal life-situations, an unrelated man would never have been so rude.

They then helped her slowly get to her feet, amidst a lot of groaning, and step into the room. She took only one step and then collapsed. The rest of the family and Wun-sik had trouble getting past her.

Mrs. Lee, a very resourceful person, had heard the unusual voices with the variety of pitch and the one word, "Moo-jee-moo." This precipitated a chain-reaction, and quickly drinks were ready for all. She had peeked through the finger-hole in the paper-door in order to count the number of children. Every paper-door in Korea that wasn't brand-new featured at least one of these convenient holes, made by some curious soul, who simply wet a finger and pressed it through the mulberry-bark paper.

By this time, Wun-yung's Mother regained her composure enough to introduce herself and her four children, apologizing profusely for being such a nuisance.

"Yes, Lee Mawk-sah," Kee-haw volunteered, "we were talking on the way here about bringing an ox-cart on the next trip. When anyone gets tired, he or she can ride awhile without delaying everyone. The trip seems to get shorter for those of us who come often. But Wun-yung's Mother's feet just aren't used to rough, gravel roads."

To this, Wun-sik politely added, "Lee Mawk-sah, it's time for you to be at the church. Please don't let us keep you any longer."

As Lee stood up to leave, thoughtful Soon-hee expressed what everyone was thinking, "Please thank your sweet wife for the wonderful drinks. The long walk is worth it for her refreshments alone."

Wun-yung, Kee-haw, Soon-hee, and Wun-sik picked up their bundles of Bible and hymnbook wrapped in napkin-like cloths, and all eight followed Lee Pastor over to the church.

One of the elders who believed in punctuality had already announced the first hymn for the opening exercises of Sunday School. As they took their places in their classes, all, except the smaller children and Wun-yung's Mother, bowed their heads. They asked God's blessing on the teacher, the lesson and the class. Then they found their place in the hymnals and started singing with the others.

CHAPTER XIV
Wun-sik Proposes

The afternoon worship service began at two o'clock. But it was nearly three-thirty when the Moo-jee-moo church-goers assembled at the Great-Gate of the churchyard to start heading home.

Wun-sik spoke up first, "You know, I had a chance to see Ahn Mawk-sah for a few minutes right after the Service. He told me that Ahn Lady wanted to see me. Her four children keep her pretty close to the house and another is on the way. Especially on Sundays she tries to leave the Korean help free to attend the services of their choice. I don't know how long it will take. If it's not too long, I might even catch up with you before you reach home. But anyway, don't wait for me. All I ask is that you please go slowly and rest often. In this way, maybe Wun-yung's Honorable Mother won't have too much discomfort."

Wun-sik hurried up the public lane that cut across the mission-station property near the southern end. It was much shorter than going around north of the hospital and up through Ahn's private gate-quarters. At the brow of the hill, he entered the gate going north, passing four missionary homes, before he came to Ahn's.

Ahn Lady had been waiting for him and answered the door herself. She bowed graciously, "You are most welcome, Naw Teacher," she greeted him. "I hope this isn't too inconvenient and doesn't delay your return home too much. I know it's a long way to Moo-jee-moo. My husband has been telling me about the wonderful ways in which our Savior has been blessing you, your friends and the village. I am most interested and concerned. I only wish I were freer and could help more. I have met you in my husband's study, but only in passing.

Please rest your mind, Naw Teacher, and tell me if there is something I can do to help."

During the latter part of her remarks, a maid had come into the parlor with two steaming hot cups of parched barley-tea. It was served in two European-style teacups with handles and a saucer under each.

Wun-sik paused to admire them. "Is everything in the Beautiful Country as dainty and pretty as these?" he asked. "I'm not ignoring your very kind offer, Ahn Lady, but they are so nice." He lifted the cup to his lips.

"Tell me about Soon-hee-ssee. She is very sweet. Of course I've seen her with Kee-haw-ssee many times," Ahn Pastor's wife remarked, "because my eldest son has matured enough recently to watch the other three children, allowing me to attend the Worship Service in the church more reguarly. I see Soon-hee almost every Sunday, and have many chances to chat with her. She is so dear. I love her very much.

"Now, to answer your question, we don't use these cups very much, for neither of us enjoy tea or coffee. But we're glad we brought them with us to Korea for our guests' sake. I'm so happy you like them.

"I mentioned Soon-hee-ssee," she went on, "Because Ahn Mawk-sah has been keeping me informed of your interest in her. You know, I've been thinking that it might be possible that talking with a woman who is close to Soon-hee-ssee might be of some help to you. I would imagine that it is difficult to talk to her husband about her!"

"I have talked to him some," Wun-sik answered Ahn Lady. "But you are right; there is a natural reticence about telling everything. I can't blame him. After all, we all have a right to a certain privacy, don't you think?"

"Yes, of course, and then don't you think that a woman sees things from a different angle? True, this is none of my business. And you don't have to listen to one word unless you want to," Ahn Lady reassured him.

"Oh, no, no! Please feel free to tell me anything and everything. You can't possibly tell what an awful feeling I have to be so much in the dark, when so much depends on the light, on knowing the truth. The Master, himself, said He was the Truth and the Light, didn't He? You are his servant, so please illumine me, Lady of Peace*," he finished. Then as an afterthought he added, "You know. I've even cultivated the eldest son's friendship. I hired him to help me in the fields, just hoping against hope that I would learn more about her!"

"Wun-sik-ssee, I believe the first thing you should know is that Soon-hee-ssee is pregnant. You may have considered the possibility, but now you know the fact. Kee-haw may be your best friend, but men are funny sometimes and don't put themselves in others' straw-shoes," she confided. "I wouldn't tell this to anyone else because it's no one else's business."

"Again you are right, Ahn Lady," Wun-sik agreed. "You are not only a Lady of Peace, but a Lady of Understanding. This was part of my darkness. Thank-you for enlightening me."

"Another thing, you may never fully know how Soon-hee-ssee has been torn by this whole matter," Ahn Lady continued. "Her love goes deep, and to that depth she has been torn. Don't expect her to change this profound affinity quickly or easily. That too will be traumatic! Tenderness and infinite patience alone will bring her through this transfer. And the little one will be her solace and her healing ointment!

"You must understand and accept this, Wun-sik-ssee. God has been very good to her in providing this little one, just when her need was so great. This will be a tremendous challenge to you and your Christian love and manhood! It will not be easy, I'm sure; but the prize will be worth the price.

"Do you have some questions or something else you want to talk about, Wun-sik-ssee? If not, I think that is about all I felt I should share with you," she concluded.

"Oh, thank you, thank you, Ahn Lady. The possibility of a child was one of my main problems. But now I see God's wonderful plan. Thank you, thank you. May I drop in next Sunday morning before the Bible Class? My dumb farm animals don't seem to understand why their Sunday evening meal is often so much later than their other evening meals."

"I'll save that time just for you, Wun-sik-ssee. God be near you all through this week. We will be lifting you often in our hearts, minds and prayers. Return in peace," said the little lady from another land.

As far as Wun-yung's Honorable Mother was concerned, the whole day had been a disaster! Why had she ever let the family talk her into that long walk to the Eup? She should never have listened to them. Let those who enjoyed trudging trudge. She was a homebody. The other side of their village, a five to ten minute walk, was enough for her. Or maybe a once-a-year walk to their fields, especially in the spring, when the grandmother flowers* were out.

The trip back from the church to their home was not quite so bad as the morning's trip. Whenever they passed a grassy hillock, the group stopped and gave her a chance to sit down, to take the weight off her feet. Different members of the family talked to her during such interludes, and this helped her forget her blisters.

When they finally got home, everyone insisted on her lying down immediately, while they assumed the supper preparation and any other chores. Little by little, Wun-yung's Mother realized that after a long soak in hot water, her feet were not really so sore. In time, her memory of the awful trip was not so painful. From reveling in self-pity, she began to revel in the idea that her whole family was so sweet and thoughtful.

Everything that needed to be done was getting done. Every single member was busy, busy, doing something useful and beneficial. For what seemed to her the first time in her life, she was just lying back and enjoying it all! What luxury! How fortunate she was! She didn't even sit up to eat supper, but leaned on one elbow and managed. Soon-hee and Sayt-jjae got up and stepped down into the kitchen, when anything was needed. What a nice family she had! If it could just go on like this forever! Maybe it wouldn't hurt to let them know how she was feeling, or would it spoil them? Maybe she should take a chance!

"You know," she began, "I was complaining a lot on the road, going and coming, but you helped me a great deal. I probably could have endured without so much fuss. And since getting home, every one of you has been so helpful. I never had it so nice in my life before. I was just thinking how lucky I am. Thank you, each one of you."

Third had just turned six a few weeks previously. She was looking forward to starting school early next spring, at the beginning of the next school year. At this juncture, not able to contain herself any longer, she piped up, "Oh, Mommie, I never heard you talk like that before! It makes me feel so good somewhere inside here," and she touched a hand to her chest. "We always love to help you, Mommie; you should lie down whenever you get tired and let us take care of you. Isn't that right, everybody?" She looked around the circle to see if her unrehearsed speech met with approval.

Little Wun-bawg-ee was clapping his hands, jumping up and down, and shouting, "That's right! That's right!"

The two older boys were caught off guard. They felt naturally that they hadn't been as helpful as they might have been in the women's department of the kitchen. So both were staring at the floor and squirming.

Kee-haw smiled broadly as he approved of his daughter's suggestion, "Good for you, Third. That's the kind of talk I like to hear."

But Soon-hee really capped it off, "How right you are, Sayt-jjae. You said what we were all thinking. If we haven't said much, it's only because we're ashamed that we haven't helped before now as much as we could have. And maybe we haven't been as cheerful about what we **have** done as you have, bless your heart!"

Kee-haw scrubbed up rather early the next Wednesday evening, before the Bible Class began. He had eaten his supper, and was reviewing his Sunday notes. His Bible lay open on the floor of the awn-dawl room of the cottage, where they usually met. He could get away from the household noises there, while preparing to teach the Bible Class. Sometimes these new believers asked some difficult questions. Several were almost as smart as Wun-sik. Kee-haw welcomed the challenge that the class brought him, as well as the study of the Word that it required of him. Tonight they were going to move over to the Big House. Wun-sik had mentioned the idea to Wun-yung's Honorable Mother, and she hadn't forgotten. In fact, she had spent most of the day cleaning up and dusting and puttering around the sah-rahng, or men's parlor.

The parlor was not as big as the family living room, but the group could easily fit in the space. And since the men and women met together, it was a nicer place.

Just then Blackie, the dog, announced a visitor, even before the usual throat-scraping. Kee-haw almost automatically resented the interruption. He needed every minute possible for his preparation. In an hour, or maybe less, they'd be coming. Why did this have to happen to him? By then he had stood up, stepped out onto the porch, and was slipping into his shoes on the stoop. But he turned and noticed that Wun-yung-ee was already at the gate. He paused, hoping that he wouldn't have to go any farther.

Much to his surprise, as soon as Wun-yung-ee opened the gate, his friend, Wun-sig-ee stepped in. Kee-haw thought, "Of all people, he should have known better. I wonder what it's all about!" Wun-sik thanked Wun-yung and then walked straight over to Kee-haw.

"Look here, Kee-haw-yah," he said, "I know that this is a bad time for you, just before the class, but after the class it's late and everyone is tired. Anyway, I don't want to see you. Go on back to your preparation. All I want is to have a little time with Soon-hee-ssee.

"On Sunday," Wun-sik continued, obviously needing to talk to his friend, "Ahn Mawk-sah's Lady helped me to do some straight thinking. I've done very little farm work since then, and when I have, my mind has not been on the work. I know my mind, but I don't know hers. According to our ancient and worthy custom, I should be talking, just as you did, to a go-between. But Kee-haw-yah, all three of us are Christians, or very nearly so. When God is in our hearts, directing us, we are not trying to drive a good bargain at someone else's expense. We simply want God's perfect will to be done, which, of course, will be the best for everyone involved.

"So, when can I talk to Soon-hee-ssee? I know that this is a very personal matter, and it would be nice to be by ourselves, but that is of secondary importance. I've decided that when the Great God puts it into our hearts to do something, we have no business dawdling."

"I'll get Soon-hee right away, Wun-sig-ee; just come inside here and sit down. I'll get my Bible and notes and find a place in the Big House where I can study a little more, and I'll be praying, too, for you and Soon-hee," Kee-haw offered, and ran across the courtyard.

Soon-hee, in the meantime, had caught fragments of the not-too-well-muted conversation. It had given her time to dry her hands, take off her apron and with both hands whisk back her hair. She was composed and ready when Kee-haw appeared at the kitchen door. "What is it?" she asked.

"I think God is answering prayers, Paw-bae-yah," he cupped his hand and whispered in her ear. "Come on over."

When they arrived at the cottage, Wun-sik had already thoughtfully gathered up the Bible and notes. He handed them to Kee-haw. Soon-hee just stood there, hands clasped together, head bowed and eyes downcast. Kee-haw sensed her diffidence and shyness. At the same time, the poignancy of the moment hit him full force. He laid his books on the porch, and tears streaming down his manly face, he held her to him very tightly for awhile. Then he gently drew her to the stoop. "Paw-bae-yah, Precious Jewel," was all he could whisper, as he helped her up the step onto the porch. Without another word, Kee-haw left the two there, took his books and went over to the other house.

Realizing something of the proprieties and her natural reticence, Wun-sik sat down on the porch and invited her to do the same. "We can talk softly, and no one will hear us," he said. His voice was very kind and quiet. Whether it was that or Kee-haw's parting caress, or her own pent-up emotions, or all three, Soon-hee, too, could no longer keep back the tears.

Wun-sik, understandingly, said: "Soon-hee-ssee, please cry all you please. Sometimes we need to 'let down the mind*,' and let the emotions go. Others will be arriving before very long, so if you don't mind and can hear me, I will talk. If this is all right with you, please just nod your head in assent."

Soon-hee gave her nod and Wun-sik continued, "Soon-hee-ssee, you may never have heard this before, as Kee-haw may not have mentioned it. During bygone years, whenever I got romantic notions, I would somehow manage to walk past your father's Great-Gate. I had hopes that I would be lucky enough to catch a glimpse of you, or hear the lilt of your happy, laughing voice, or see your braid of glossy, black hair. I didn't always see you, but if I did, my spirits rose to High Heaven for days to come.

"Of course, I never expected to be rich enough to marry you, as did Kee-haw. But in my dreamier moments, I even thought of that possibility. That, however, was before any of us were Christians, or even considered accepting The Faith. I'm simply telling you this to let you know that even when my own wife was living, and I had no Christian ideals, I was strongly attracted to you. I felt that you were the most winsome and lovely girl in town."

By now Soon-hee had fairly well gotten herself under control, with only an occasional catching of her breath in a little sob. She was listening very intently to every word and wondering if any other Korean girl had ever had a man tell her such beautiful things before they were married.

"A few weeks ago," Wun-sik continued, "Kee-haw confided in me about your problems as Christians in a dual-wife marriage. He told me that he was looking for a suitable man to be your husband. Naturally, I looked back into my own heart and wondered whether now, with clear conscience, I might still aspire to your hand. God has been very good to give me the answers to some questions that came to mind. So now I feel that with my whole heart, I can offer myself to you. If this is too sudden and doesn't allow enough time to consider all the aspects, I will be patient and wait for your answer. But," he whispered, "please, don't take too long! I love you, Soon-hee-ssee, with all my heart!"

Without the slightest bit of false modesty, Soon-hee pulled back her crisp, cotton skirt and wiped her eyes and delicate nose on her white petticoat. "You are a very thoughtful, kind and good-looking young man, Wun-sik-ssee. God has been good to cross our paths. I am so fortunate that you and my husband have been exposed to the Christian teachings, so that both of you are considering my wishes and welfare as well. Even in Korea, women have minds of their own, you know. Since realizing that my present way of life could not go on indefinitely, I too have been wondering about and most, of all, praying for God's choice. I have combined this with a deep trust that our gracious Father would provide and lead me to the right man.

"I can very well understand that you want my answer quickly, yet time is so unimportant where matters of the heart are concerned. A short moment may be a year! You know full well, Wun-sik-ssee, that my heart is badly torn. I like you, yes; in fact, a big yes! I like your humor, I like your considerateness, I like your cheerfulness, I like your laugh, I like your Christian gentility and gentleness. I like your sincerity; in fact, there is very little I don't like about you.

"Wun-sik-ssee, you deserve more than a torn and bleeding heart. I have gone through quite a bit of hell here, but thank God, I have also had a lot of Heaven. So please give me a few moments to let Heaven heal, and I'll try to give you an answer that is worthy of your love," Soon-hee completed her reply. At that moment Blackie announced some footsteps in the lane, approaching the Great-Gate.

"Please excuse me, Wun-sik-ssee, I'm probably needed over on the other side of the mah-dahng. But remember, your words will forever peal in my heart, and I'm sure the healing won't take too long!" She donned her shoes and ran across the courtyard to the outside kitchen door, her face aglow!

Wun-sik sauntered over to the sah-rahng outer door and scraped his throat. Kee-haw had heard Blackie's bark, and more or less subconsciously had registered the fact that his preparation must finish shortly. His friend's signal confirmed this. He rose and threw the door open. By then, Wun-yung had raced out to and opened the Great-Gate, and several people were walking over to the cottage.

Kee-haw had begun to ask Wun-sik about the conversation, but out of the corner of his eye he saw the others going the wrong way. Quick as a flash, he switched tracks, saying, "Just a minute, Wun-sik . . . ." Then he raised his voice and called, "You folks! Please come over here! This evening we're going to meet in a new place." They looked surprised but reversed their steps.

There was no time now to find out anything from Wun-sik, so Kee-haw stepped back from the door to let him enter. The others soon followed, each one ducking a head under the low lintel, as he or she came through the door.

After everyone had arrived, the class began. Kee-haw said, "Some of you may be wondering why we're meeting over here this evening. The room is larger for one thing, but that's not the primary reason. Wun-yung's Honorable Mother is not such a bad housekeeper, if I say it myself. Please don't repeat this, but our family is proud of her. Last Sunday, she accompanied us to the Church Service in the Eup. She, herself, invited us to meet here in the sah-rahng, and I'm sure we're very happy to do so. In fact, if I'm not mistaken, she may even honor us with her presence after she tidies up the kitchen."

CHAPTER XV
A Certain Satisfaction

Kee-haw led in the opening prayer. He prayed very earnestly that God would help each of them to look deeply into his own heart. He asked God to expose anything of any sort that was blocking the fullness of God's blessing from their lives. Then he added two other requests: first, that God would help each of them to have the grace and courage to rid himself of the blockage, and second, if anyone had been hurt or harmed, that proper restitution would be made to him or her.

Several of them had only recently joined the class. But they had quickly learned that prayers were ended with an "Amen," whatever that meant. Kee-haw felt a certain satisfaction in hearing them all audibly join in this closing word. Somehow he felt that this, in a way, indicated that they were making some progress in this new life of the Spirit.

"Now friends," he began, "this Christian life that we are studying from God's Word is nothing, unless it is lived out. I mean that it means sacrifice; we must OBEY WHAT WE READ AND WHAT WE LEARN, IN EVERY PART OF OUR LIVES. It's quite possible that some of you or some of your friends in Moo-jee-moo have some doubts. You may be wondering, in fact, how I can even try to lead a Bible Class week by week when the Bible teachs monogamy, and I have two wives. And this is a legitimate question.

"As you well know, none of us knew anything of the Jesus-Way when this dual-wife relationship was negotiated. As you also know, I was the first one to attend the Sunday morning Bible Classes in the Eup. For the first few months, I didn't know that the Jesus-Teaching taught that monogamy was God's will for everyone. Many of the Eup-people who were members of the Adult Class had only seen me on market-days.

Even then they had only thought of me as an unlettered country-jake. Of late, Ahn Mawk-sah has helped to change that impression. Of course they have seen Soon-hee-ssee going to church with me during the last few months. But none of them realized that she wasn't my First-Wife, and they have been too polite to inquire.

"So it was almost by accident that I discovered this teaching of God's Word a few months ago. Lee Mawk-sah and Ahn Mawk-sah have both been very helpful. They have spent many hours and much effort trying to unravel our mistakes in such a way that the fewest people would be hurt, and those as little as possible.

"If any of you have any suggestions that would help, please feel free to communicate. We are trying to keep open to God's leading, keeping in mind that many times He uses people to help each other. Now unless there is something that someone has to say, we'll begin our lesson for the evening."

Soon-hee had come in late from the kitchen. Since there was only a paper door between the two rooms, she had heard almost every word of Kee-haw's. "Excuse me, good husband," she added. "I know you want to get to the lesson. What I have to say will take but a minute, and I think this is probably the best time. I really believe that my Outside-Lord* is the best husband that ever lived. God was very good to me to let me have him even for this short time, and even as his Second-Wife. My husband has asked you to help us straighten out our complexities. After all, we are one family of God's children, and if we don't help each other, we're not a very good family. So I want to add that my husband is right. We need your help. And if you will help us, maybe we can bring a little glory to God out of our big mess."

Humbly her eyes dropped to the floor, and several big tears rolled down her cheeks, as she finished, "Please, please help us. I think that Christians must be a community of members who help each other, especially when we go wrong."

Wun-yung's Honorable Mother had slipped in quietly during Soon-hee's remarks. Without really standing up, she had unobtrusively sidled into a nearby corner of the room. Everyone realized that this was the first time she had ever come and sat down with them, that is, with the evident purpose of studying the Bible. They purposely avoided looking at her, not wanting to embarrass, but their faces couldn't help lighting up. From her corner it was no great feat to glance quietly around the room. She immediately concluded from the happy faces that Bible study must be very, very pleasant.

An hour or so later most of the villagers had left, that is, all except Wun-sik. Kee-haw had stepped out into the mahdahng to bid farewell to some of his friends. Wun-sik realized that there was no chance for him to talk to Soon-hee alone, surrounded as they were by paper-doors. So he soon followed Kee-haw.

"Say, Kee-haw-yah, how in the world do you remember so much from the Sunday Bible Class? I don't believe that I could have recalled half of what you did! But I got just as good grades as you did in the old 'Writing Room*,' " he commented.

"I wish that were really true, my friend," Kee-haw parried, "but thanks just the same. For the last half-year or so, I've been jotting some brief notes and specially significant words. You know, anything that I feel might be of interest and value to our group. By the way, Wun-sig-ee, I'd feel a lot better if someone else taught our class here, especially until I get my family affairs straightened out. Why don't you take over for awhile? I know you haven't been attending church in the Eup very long. But with your education and your sincerity as well as your passion to improve yourself for Soon-hee's sake, I believe you'd do very well."

"What are you talking about, Kee-haw-yah? Have your senses flown out the window? Why I'm just a baby when it comes to the knowledge of Christian Truth!" Wun-sik exclaimed.

"Now, there's no need to get so excited, friend. Can't you let me think out loud with my best friend? But I am very serious about this, Wun-sig-ee. You can come over as early as you want every Wednesday evening. I'll be glad to give you as much time as you need to compare my notes with yours. And I'll try to explain anything that isn't quite clear to you, if I can. Please consider this. It would mean a great deal to me. I would feel a lot better, and I believe that God would honor us for making this change." Kee-haw did his best to alter Wun-sik's attitude.

"Well, that's different, if you put it that way, friend; but let me try it for a time or two, and if it just doesn't work, you're going to have to take it back again. Promise me, you rascal, or I won't even do it once," Wun-sik returned.

He then walked back several paces toward the outside kitchen door which stood slightly ajar. He called in, "Wun-yung's Honorable Mother, it was so nice meeting in your very nice sah-rahng. You are an artist at keeping everything nicely put away. We should have thought of this long ago. By the way, this husband fellow of yours is quite a man. I've been trying to tell him so, but he's turned the tables on me. Imagine, he's trying to coax me into teaching the class. Can you believe that? He needs a paddling on the two spots provided for such purposes!

"Please sleep in peace, all of you. And please tell that other nice lady, wherever she is, that I am anxious to get home and get to sleep. I know that I am going to have the most delectable and elegant dreams I have ever had." As Kee-haw walked with him to the Great-Gate, Wun-sik said, "Come outside the gate a minute, Kee-haw-yah." They both stepped high over the cross-piece at the bottom of the little door, built into the left one of the two big doors. Wun-sik then pulled the little door shut.

"Kee-haw-yah," he began, "I proposed to Soon-hee-ssee this evening. It might have seemed rather sudden to her. At any rate, she asked for time for God to heal her torn and bleeding heart. Now, here's the remarkable thing: she didn't ask for much time, only a few moments. Actually, she has had much more than a few moments already. I know it's a little late, though the sun sets earlier these days. I don't want to thoughtlessly go home if she is waiting for me to resume the conversation. What do you think?"

Kee-haw said, "Just wait here, Wun-sig-ee, I'll go and ask her. She'll doubtless know what she wants." He stepped back into the mah-dahng and walked over to the one-room-and-lean-to-cottage. Then he called, "Yu-baw*." Soon-hee came to the outside kitchen-door, opened it wide and stepped out.

"Yes," she answered.

"Come here a minute, Soon-hee," he requested. Voice considerably lowered, he said, "Soon-hee, Wun-sik is waiting outside the Great-Gate. He felt that maybe there is some unfinished business between you two, and he didn't want to thoughtlessly go on home if there was. He could come here if you want him to, and you two could talk on the porch. What is your wish?"

Soon-hee came very close and spoke in little more than a whisper, "Master, we have both faced this thing squarely and pretty well decided there is only one thing to do. I know there is no use talking about torn hearts. God will heal when we are ready and willing and if we do what is right. Dawdling will only prolong the agony, and this is not God's way.

"An hour or two ago I asked for the healing of High Heaven. I've had the time, and I think the healing is coming, for you and me and for the whole family. God is good. He's the One who put it in the heart of Wun-yung's Honorable Mother to go with us to church last Sunday. And He's the One who brought her into our Bible Class tonight. He's the One who is changing all of us so that our lives will be more unselfishly pleasant and pleasure-giving.

"I say, 'Yes' with all my heart. Since Wun-sik-ssee thought of it himself, and God has put it in our hearts, please ask him to come back in."

Kee-haw quickly went back to the Great-Gate, but to his consternation, Wun-sik was nowhere in sight. It was a black, black night and Kee-haw knew that his friend wouldn't have had to move far to melt into the darkness, even if he were dressed in his long, white too-roo-mahk*, as he was. He took the eight long paces to the corner of the lane on the run, almost running into Wun-sik who was coming back to the Gate.

"Where have you been, you good-for-nothing rascal?" Kee-haw blurted out.

"Oh, I just thought I'd step over to the corner and look down the long stretch of lane, to see if by any chance someone might be snooping around. But you can't see ten chah* in front of your nose tonight," Wun-sik replied. "What's the grand rush anyway?"

"Nothing at all. It just startled me to have you suddenly vanish on such a dark night," Kee-haw answered. "Yes, Soon-hee wants to see you, and I suggested that her porch is probably the best place. That's where you talked awhile ago."

Together they turned back to the Gate. Kee-haw continued, "You know, Wun-sik, I, for one, am finding that the laws of God are immutable. In ignorance and selfishness, we failed to observe one important law of God. Even before we knew why, each member of our family felt some unhappy result of our mistake. Now that we know better, we are doing better, and happiness and healing are returning. Isn't that wonderful? And you, my good and best friend, are part of it all."

By then they had reached the porch. Kee-haw observed, "Sorry we took so long, Soon-hee; I thought for a few minutes that we had lost this very nice gentlemen. You know, Soon-hee, I was just thinking, I could have traveled the world and hunted for years and years and never found a better man than Wun-sik, nor a man who would be nicer to you. The infallible laws of God say that as Christians, you and I can't have each other. Since this is true, I don't know of anyone that I'd rather see have you as his wife than Wun-sik." He turned on his heel, saying, "If Wun-yung's still up, I'll send him over with a lantern. I never saw a darker night!"

Wun-sik went up on the porch. Soon-hee had been seated, but she arose and with outstretched hands walked over to Wun-sik, saying, "I'm so happy you stayed. Please sit down. Let me get you a cushion." She went inside and reappeared shortly with two thin cushions. Wun-yung was coming across the mah-dahng, adjusting the lantern's* wick till it gave a nice clear light.

Wun-yung slipped out of his shoes and came up on the porch. He placed the lantern in the darkest corner. Then he turned to Soon-hee who had seated herself on the other side of the porch across from Wun-sik. He walked over to her, turned to Wun-sik with an "Excuse me," then turned back to Soon-hee. Cupping his hand to her ear, he whispered very softly, "I think he's a good man, but are you sure he's the one for you, Little Mother?" She smiled very sweetly, then nodded her head affirmatively. He waited a moment, then whispered again, "Look, you don't have to give your answer tonight. It won't hurt to sleep over it."

Again she smiled and then added, "Thank you, Wun-yung-ee." The lad then bowed to Wun-sik and went back over to the big house.

Soon-hee opened the conversation. "It is unseemly for me, a woman, to speak first, but I have kept you waiting, Wun-sik-ssee, for too long already. Please forgive me. It was not intentional. The evening has just been very full."

"That's all right, Soon-hee-ssee; I understand. Please go right ahead," Wun-sik returned.

"Only a few minutes ago I was sharing with Kee-haw something of the wonderful way in which our lovely Heavenly Father is bringing healing to me. I asked you to allow me a few moments to let Heaven heal, and sure enough, in a very few moments, Wun-yung's Honorable Mother came in to study in our Bible Class for the first time. Thus did our merciful Father bring healing both to Kee-haw-ssee and to me. Wasn't that marvelous?

"Thus did He also give His stamp of approval on our new and untried love. We can know that Wun-yung's Honorable Mother will be a good wife to Kee-haw and liberate me, without guilt, to be yours*. Kee-haw has been so good to me during our short marriage. I could not think of leaving him without being sure of this.

"Now, Wun-sik-ssee, above and beyond these other things is our Heaven-given LOVE for each other. You are a most wonderful man! God used you in large part to break through to the person that the rest of us had never seen, that person hidden inside Wun-yung's Honorable Mother. Now it is blossoming, and I love you for this. You are a most wonderful man! And this is only one of many different ways in which God has revealed to me how **wonderful** you are and what a **very** good husband you will be to me.

"I'm going to tell you something now, Wun-sik-ssee, that I have never said to another living soul. Usually we women think that a man's handsomeness is primarily in his face. I haven't had a chance to tell you until now. On our long walks to and from church, I have discovered the character that shows up in your strong, straight back, it's almost as much as in your face. And this is true in the handsome things you think of to do for people.

"Right from the beginning, I'm going to promise you something with all my heart. I will steadfastly avoid comparing you with the only other man I have ever known. I will avoid this even in my innermost thinking, let alone my spoken word. Of course, that's not counting my father. Somehow I have a very deep feeling that no possible good could come from such comparisons."

After Kee-haw had sent Wun-yung over with the lantern, he hadn't gone into the house-proper. The poor neglected cow had been politely grumbling for her dinner of chook* for some time. Kee-haw apologized to her as he dipped it out of the large cauldron and poured it into her own cracked but mended pot. He gave her a kindly pat on the forehead. He called in through the paper door to the living/dining room that he might be a little late getting in. Then he slipped out the back gate. He wasn't sure just where he was going. He only knew he had to get away, away by himself, to get himself together!

So far, it had been mostly his mind and his good sense that had agreed with this dramatic change in his life. But it was going to have to be more than that. He would have to accept the change with his entire being, and he knew now that he was more than mind and sense. He was heart and body, and soul. And his emotions were churning in his breast.

Now, how was he going to get himself together? Well certainly not at home, with people everywhere! Was it habit or some inner compulsion that was taking him out to his fields, these fields that furnished his family with food and life? Maybe it didn't matter what it was. Maybe this wasn't the time to try to answer that one. At any rate, here were the fields, his fields, his family's fields. Yes, for generations back his ancestors and their beasts of burden had added their sweat and their droppings to this wonderful soil. It was rich, it was fertile, it was theirs. He stooped and let a handful run easily through his fingers. Even Soon-hee, blessed woman, for a time at least, had been considered to be deserving of the produce of these fields.

Yes, for her sake and for the sake of their son yet unborn, he would take her a large sack of his best rice every fall. For many years to come, as long as she had life in that precious body, he would do this. He must talk to Wun-sik and to Wun-yung about his decision. Yes, it was only fair and right that he do this much or more.

He sat for awhile on one of the un-duk* while these and other thoughts galloped through his mind. Wasn't it good he'd taken time out to come out here? Somehow he was thinking more clearly when nothing else confused his thoughts. What would his son or daughter be named? In time, would he want to go to a Great School* and prepare to become a famous doctor, just like the one in the Mission Hospital in the Eup? He had heard that if the doctor had stayed and practiced in the Beautiful Country, he could have become a rich man. There must be something very magnificent in a man who would do that for some poor people he didn't even know!

Well, things were beginning to come together. He was happy to have thought of that yearly bag of rice. Of course, he would hull it and polish it before he took it over. Which brought up the thought, "It won't be too long till harvest time this fall. Some of the fields have a slight yellow tint already."

Out loud, right there on the paddy-dike, he said, "I'll take the first sack over before Christmas. Won't that be a surprise? Then I'll talk with Wun-sig-ee about the future. After all, the little fellow will be here before transplanting season next year. My goodness, time and birthdays don't wait for anyone, do they?"

He had to work tomorrow, so maybe he ought to get some rest tonight. Over there in the village, what was that sleepy rooster doing, crowing before midnight? But before going back, he'd stand up and stretch and wander over to the family graveyard, or as much of one as they had. Of course, there were graves of the family which extended far up the mountain, graves at propitious sites, chosen by the moo-nyu*. There were only two graves in this nearby site. And now, since his family members were Christians for whom it was not necessary to go back to the moo-nyu any more, this site was roomy enough. It would serve their family's needs for a generation or two.

Kee-haw sat on his mother's grave for awhile. She had died three years after his father, who died six years ago, and she'd been only forty-four years old. Of course that was before they built the Western Hospital in the Eup. If any of them had had enough sense, she could have gone to the missionary doctor for some Western yahk*. Well, in the old days if herb-doctors and moo-nyu, didn't have the right herbs for a certain disease, it was just too bad. The patient died, no matter how young.

Kee-haw stood up. He had run away from everything long enough. Maybe he wasn't exactly all together, but at least he was in better shape than he had been two or three hours ago. Wun-sig-ee had probably gone on home some time ago, and Kee-haw guessed that the only place for him now was the big house. He must keep his relationships clear-cut and straight from now on. He started back through his fields.

"The first thing in the morning," he said to himself, "before Wun-sik has gone out to the fields, I'll run over and see him. Perhaps he'd like to get an early start, too, and go with me in to see Ahn Pastor and set a date for the wedding." It shouldn't take too long, if they got a good early start and really walked fast. They should be back on their farms by nine-thirty or ten.

Even on that familiar path back through his fields and then on to his home, Kee-haw found himself stumbling badly! It was almost as though he were drunk! Maybe he hadn't gotten himself together as well as he thought. He had made up his mind to go back to the big house. Were his feet refusing to cooperate? Maybe deep somewhere inside of himself something, some part of him, was saying, "NO; NO! How can I relinquish the only real JOY, the only real sunshine and light I have ever had? What am I doing? How can a man tear the very heart right out of himself and go on living?"

He stumbled badly again. This time he almost went to his knees. He happened to touch the front of his vest. It was his nice vest that he'd put on for the meeting and forgotten to take off, and it was sopping wet. Had he been crying that long? Maybe that, combined with the pitch-blackness, was why he was stumbling so badly!

Again he heard that crazy rooster crowing! Was the whole world topsy-turvy or was it just that young scratchy-voiced rooster and he? Or was the night really almost gone and he only a befuddled fool?

CHAPTER XVI
A Church Wedding

Another two-and-a-half weeks had slowly crept by. It was the first Sunday that Ahn Mawk-sah could come. The word that the Western Pastor was there reached the villagers again. Evening service was filled with people. Afterward, everyone went home, that is, everyone except Ahn Mawk-sah, sweet Soon-hee and Wun-sik. One little ceramic kerosene lamp shone on the pulpit, the round wick no larger than a fairly stout cotton string. The light flickered badly, as the fitful fall breezes found their way through the little foot-square windows.

Kee-haw was the first one out of the door, following the Service. He had one or two chores that needed to be done. He completed them, and, supperless, retraced his steps to the chapel. He walked rather slowly, because he didn't want to meet anyone going home and have to fend off a barrage of unwanted questions.

Again he was almost blinded by tears. But this time with a firm step, he found his way through the black shadows of the familiar village lanes. Entering the church courtyard, he went to the back door on the men's side of the meeting-house.

No one knew that poor Kee-haw, in his stocking feet, had slipped in. He was determined to see this thing through to the end, yes, the bitter end.

The marriage ceremony was just getting under way. Kee-haw had time to think, "Wun-sik is getting a true gem. The last few months, she has matured so rapidly, and especially since she became pregnant. Also since she started attending Service with me in the Eup, she is so much more companionable than at first. She's the one now who thinks of all the little ways to make life easier for First-Wife. Yes, though I can hardly believe it, First-Wife is going to miss her almost as much as I." Copious tears were still streaming.

By now, Ahn was reading the marriage vows. His voice was clear and strong. At this moment he was intoning, "Whom God hath joined together, let no man put asunder." The minister's words carried a deeper portent than usual. "Soon-hee-ssee and Wun-sik-ssee," he said, "nowhere in God's Word does it say, 'Marry the woman or the man that you love.' But the Word of God does say very clearly, 'Wife, love your husband,' and 'Husband, love your wife.' Never should we let our loves rule and govern us. Rather, with the wisdom God gives us, must we direct and control these loves, so that they always bring credit to Him."

Just then Ahn looked up at the couple. His glance happened to go past them to the back of the three-kahn chapel. There in the semidarkness, he made out the dim form of Kee-haw, in his white Sunday-clothes, kneeling in the back corner of the men's side, his hands clasped as in prayer, tears streaming down his handsome face. Ahn's voice choked, as he realized the enormity of Kee-haw's loss. He was forced to pause for several minutes to gain control.

Finally he was able to look up at the couple again, smile, and continue, "Beginning then with your love as it is now, selflessly give of yourselves day by day and **many times** a day to each other. GROW in this **greatest** thing in God's world, LOVE. God bless you my children, Amen."

The three blew out the lamp and went out the front door.

In the inky blackness of the back part of the meeting-room, Kee-haw continued to kneel. For awhile, the tears also continued. He had done what was right. He had joined hands with God. He had helped God Himself to straighten out a hitherto hopeless mess!

He stayed on his knees for an hour or more in the complete darkness. The last footsteps in the village lanes had long since died away. Yes, he'd done what was right and GOD WOULD BRING PEACE UNDER HIS ROOF. The older children would certainly understand, and in her way, maybe

First-Wife would, too. She had borne him three fine sons and a very sweet daughter.

He would go back home now. Half his heart or more was dead. It felt like a lot more than half. He stepped out into the night. It was as dark outside as it had been in. To his surprise he found he was walking in a heavy drizzle.

"God understands," he said aloud. "Even Heaven weeps on such a night as this."

Through the pitch-black darkness he went. He stumbled, even on that familiar path. The biggest and the best happiness in his life was gone forever! This he knew! Would light ever come again?

"But I did what was right!" he cried. "The light must break! The PEACE MUST COME."

And then most strangely, right there in that blacker than black village lane, he realized that there was a singular lightness in the other half of his heart. He felt an unfamiliar happiness and freedom that had never been his before! GOD WAS GOOD! He had lifted the blight! He had brought the light! PEACE HAD COME.

Kee-haw stretched out his full five feet nine on the fast-drying turf. Again it was autumn in this land of Korea. The gold and scarlet zelkova leaves were again side-slipping back and forth as Kee-haw chatted with Wun-sik. A full eleven months had elapsed since Wun-sik's marriage to the sweetest girl in thirteen provinces.

Toward the end of the previous winter, a dainty little girl with lovely straight black hair had been born to Soon-hee. She and Wun-sik, with the tacit approval of Kee-haw, had named her Pawk-soon. Little Pawk-soon had captured the hearts of both families. But Soon-hee was determined not to let them spoil her seven-month-old daughter.

It was Sunday afternoon, about four-thirty, still a little early to tend to the evening chores. Wun-sik was talking, "Kee-haw-yah, you know my family is still pretty small and my crops are doing well. It was really munificent of you to bring me that big sack of nicely polished rice last fall. However, don't you think that one is enough?"

"Now, Wun-sig-ee. Let's not waste our time together bringing up closed subjects. Didn't I tell you that I vowed to the God of High Heaven that as long as Soon-hee-ssee drew breath and as long as my sons and I could till the good earth, we would deliver a large sack of well-polished rice to you every fall? Are you trying to get me to break a promise to God? Think of it this way, Wun-sig-ee; it's a thank-you offering. I'm giving it to God for His special goodness in getting our family out of that awful mess. It's such a relief, I should really do much more than that, certainly no less," Kee-haw replied. "You just happen to be at the other end of the gift, but it's actually God who is passing it on to you, not I."

"I see your point, Kee-haw-yah, and I am grateful. Do you realize that the first anniversary of my marriage to Soon-hee is only a few weeks off? In fact it's the twenty-fourth of this coming month. Do you suppose that you and your family would like to help us celebrate? I was just thinking that all our family members have never been together or done anything nice together. What do you say?" Wun-sik queried.

"I still say you're the best friend a fellow ever had or ever will have." Then lowering his voice, Kee-haw continued, "even though you did take my favorite wife away from me, you rapscallion, you." He reached over and punched Wun-sik in the ribs. "What do I say? I say, 'You're a genius at thinking up exciting things to do. Of course you were all wrong a couple of years ago. Just how do you propose to do this celebrating?' "

"Oh, any way that would be fun for everybody. I was hoping that you would have some ideas to contribute," Wun-sik answered. "But it seems like we haven't had a good chance to share our innermost thoughts for ages, Kee-haw-yah. While you're getting some ideas together, let me interject.

"You know when Pawk-soon-ee made her arrival, early last spring, or was it late last winter, I was a little bit disappointed. Somehow, as we Korean men usually do, I'd set my heart on a boy to pal with and to help me in the fields."

"Well, God helped me to see that I was being selfish. After all, Soon-hee was the one who had had her whole life rudely interrupted. Certainly she should be rewarded with the joys and companionship of a little girl. When that was made plain to me, I was more happy than if the baby had been a boy."

"How right you are, Wise Man, I couldn't have figured it out better myself," Kee-haw agreed. "Now let's talk about your anniversary. How about our declaring a holiday for the whole day, which is a Thursday, I believe. You and I can do our early chores and even have two or three hours for field work after breakfast. It'll take the womenfolk that long to fix something nice for a late picnic up on the grassy nooks of our front mountain. The grass is still fairly green and the kids will enjoy romping around. Let's plan to eat our lunches at home at noon or even a little earlier."

"Sounds wonderful," Wun-sik agreed. "Let's take the little ones with us and meet up there on the mountain. It'll probably be about one or one-thirty, don't you think? It shouldn't take much over twenty or twenty-five minutes from either of our homes to get there. That will give us two hours or more before the older kids arrive from school. Don't you think that would be sufficient time for any adult talk that we might want to indulge in? It should be nice under the shade of those big pine trees."

"Agreed," Kee-haw returned. "Let's keep it all very quiet, so we don't have any outsiders snooping around. I'll caution the kids to keep it quiet, too."

Thursday the twenty-fourth arrived quickly. Wun-yung's Mother thought of asking Wun-yung-ee to run over to Soon-hee's several days before the Anniversary, so that she, his mother, could learn about the plans. Thus she was able to vary the picnic menu a bit and add to the food, so there would be enough for all.

They had agreed to meet at the first set of graves. On the lower slopes there was plenty of smooth wild grass where the children could play. Kee-haw had installed the big wide basket on his chee-ge so that Wun-yung's Mother didn't have to carry a thing. But it was still after one-thirty when the Paek family made it to the rendezvous.

Wun-yung's Mother immediately chose the flat, votive-offering table-stone, used on ancestral worship days. It was just the right height for a seat, and with no sense of profanity, she sat down on it. "Well, I'm sure glad it wasn't any farther," was all she said.

She had been quite faithful in her attendance at Worship in the new chapel since its erection. Prior to that, the weekly trip to the Eup had been a major battlefield. If for any reason the ox-cart didn't take her, she always came out the victor and stayed at home.

All four adults exchanged salutations. Then Kee-haw said, "It's too bad we didn't think of doing something like this sooner. As long as the sun stays out, we're all right. But if it clouds up with a north breeze, we'll want to go home, even if the kids haven't gotten here yet."

"How right you are, Kee-haw-yah," Wun-sik replied. "It's too bad we need an excuse to have a two-family picnic. A month ago, we'd have been much surer of a nice warm afternoon. If we have another picnic next fall, we'll just have to plan to have it a month before our anniversary!"

Soon-hee addressed Wun-yung's Mother, "It's so nice to see you again, Wun-yung's Honorable Mother. You are looking so fine. Have you finished filling up and burying your tawk* with the winter kim-chee?"

"Oh yes," she answered. "We harvested our persimmons* early this week, and lately we've been having early morning frosts, so it's high time to have our kim-chee tawk* filled. How about you?"

"Oh sure, we've got ours practically finished," Soon-hee replied.

"But why are we talking about kim-chee, when Pawk-soon-ee's* here? I've hardly seen her during these seven months, except when she's on your back, and you're so busy doing the laundry down at the stream." The older woman finished, "Please let me hold her for a few minutes."

Soon-hee had already loosened the broad cotton sash around her waist and slid little Pawk-soon-ee around in front. She was nursing her when the others arrived. In fact, she was still nursing her, though the little tike was showing signs of having had just about enough. Mothers, with very little veiling of their ample breasts, nursed their infants, wherever and whenever it was required. It was quite a common sight in those days, as well as for many years thereafter. A curtain down the middle of every church sanctuary gave more privacy than most mothers usually had for this normal, many-times-a-day occurrence.

Soon-hee made up Pawk-soon-ee's mind for her by detaching the baby's idle mouth from the nipple. She felt the doubled up cloth that was lying loose between her legs to see if she was dry. Then she handed her to Wun-yung's Mother, who exclaimed, "Oh, I'd forgotten that girls were so light and so sweet. I hope that she doesn't mind this new face. It's not as pretty as yours."

Soon-hee replied, "Now, never mind! You have a right to a wrinkle or two after four of them!"

Wun-yung's Mother held her hand up to the side of her mouth so the two men would not hear her next remark, "The Lord-man wasn't too happy when Pawk-soon-ee arrived on the scene, was he? Men are always that way!"

"Yes, I know, he could have been angry. But he prayed, and God told him that I needed a girl-baby, so he didn't say one cross word to me. You wouldn't believe that could happen in Korea, would you?" Soon-hee whispered back.

The older woman put her hand down and in a normal tone that all could hear, continued, "So from now on you're going to be called Pawk-soon's Mother. Do you like it?"

"Oh, yes. I'm getting quite used to it. And the name Pawk-soon is as pretty as Soon-hee anyway and has much of the same happy meaning," Soon-hee answered.

"You two men must excuse our private women's talk," Wun-yung's Mother interjected. "But here's something that will interest you. Almost every day I find something new and surprising and almost fascinating about the Jesus-Religion. For example, your attitude, Wun-sik-ssee, toward having a girl-child," Wun-yung's Mother added. "It certainly makes life more interesting and bearable. I probably don't need to tell you this, but it was only about a year ago that I felt very deeply that life was almost unendurable. Now I have moments of sheer joy, even though I have to work harder than before."

"We are so happy with you, Wun-yung's Honorable Mother," Wun-sik quickly took up the conversation. "You are truly a remarkable woman. How do you find time for all your many, many duties, and still raise your children so well? God must give you extra strength somehow, don't you think?"

"You exaggerate a thousand ten thousand times. But I must add this, Wun-sik-ssee. Kee-haw is a lot more thoughtful than he ever was before he became a Christian. Almost every day, without my saying a word, he brings me a full load of water in the two empty kerosene cans*. You know, the ones he was able to buy in the Eup. And you know as well as I that water-carrying has always been one of the female jobs in most of our land," Wun-yung's Mother responded.

Tool-jjae and Sayt-jjae had been playing around the school-yard very quietly. They did not want to attract the attention of any teachers, while they waited for Wun-yung to finish his classes. When the last bell rang he appeared. According to their prearranged plans they took the usual lane towards home, even though it was longer. After their companions had dropped out at their homes, all three of them changed their direction and headed straight for the front of the mountain.

Wun-yung-ee was ahead as they went, single-file. He also had picked up a rather quaint Korean custom on the narrow paths, talking to the air ahead of him. He even expected those following behind to hear and understand everything he said. "Daddy said that he'd bring everything we needed for the picnic. He also said that, as the days are getting shorter, we plan to finish our eating by five-thirty or so. Then we'll have time for our homework after we get home. Daddy said that he'd even do some of my evening chores to help out. Wasn't that nice?"

Tool-jjae piped up: "It sure was. We have a wonderful father, don't we?"

Not to be left out, Sayt-jjae chimed in with a "Yes we do. But you gentlemen haven't said one word about our Honorable Mommie? Remember none of us would be here if it weren't for her. And look how hard she works at home every single day, even Sundays."

"Yes, and look how nice she is to us, cooking three meals every day," Tool-jjae answered. "Haven't you noticed, both of you, how much nicer she talks to us whenever we forget something she's asked us to do. It's really true. She doesn't make us feel so bad, but I think we don't forget as much as we used to."

"Do you realize when it was that everything started to change?" Wun-yung reminded the other two. "It was before she started going to the church in the Eup, that her voice was so sharp and so hard. Since then and since she began having the Bible Class meet in the Big House, her voice has been much kinder. Look; we can see them all now through the trees. Hello-o-o-o! everybody!" he called, "here we are!"

The three of them ran the rest of the way. "Oh, look at Pawk-soon-ee, crawling on the grass. Can she stand up yet?" Sayt-jjae wanted to know. "Isn't she pretty!"

"Only if she's holding onto something that's pretty solid," Soon-hee replied.

"Oh, please, may I pick her up?" Sayt-jjae asked.

"Surely," Soon-hee answered; "but just don't walk around too much. The ground is uneven, and if you turned your ankle and fell, holding her, both of you might get hurt."

Wun-yung addressed the younger of his siblings who had just climbed the foothills with him. "Why don't you two kids play some games with Wun-bawg-ee? I'd like to listen to the big-folks-talk. Would that be all right for awhile?"

"Oh, don't worry about us," Tool-jjae responded. "Now that you're almost twelve, we understand that you must feel practically grown up. Come on Wun-bawg-ee, let us three go exploring in this big forest of trees around the graves, if we can get Sayt-jjae to put Pawk-soon-ee down for a few minutes."

Remembering his manners, Wun-yung turned to the adults. "Now that I'm older, do you mind if I stay with you and listen to your conversation? Please let me. I might grow up faster if I know how adults think and hear what they say."

"Well, son, I think I know how you feel. If Wun-sik-ssee and Pawk-soon-ee's Honorable Mother don't mind, I'm sure we don't. We're certainly not divulging great secrets out here today!" Kee-haw laughingly replied.

"I'm glad that your parents are consenting, Wun-yung-ee," Wun-sik spoke up. "Let me just say this; you're a fine young man, Wun-yung-ee, and you're kind of my partner, you know. You've put a lot of work in on my farm on Saturday afternoons. You shouldn't have to ask our permission to join our discussion. We should have thought to invite you to sit with us and take part. Please excuse us for not thinking of it first. And please feel free to express yourself. We would really appreciate your telling us what younger people are thinking nowadays."

Then turning to Wun-yung's Mother he continued, "You know, Wun-yung's Honorable Mother, everyone knows what a good wife and mother you are. You hardly ever stay around to chat after the afternoon Service. Most of the womenfolk seem to like to talk awhile before going home to prepare the next meal. The reason I mention this is that Pawk-soon's Mother and I don't have much of a chance to see and talk with you two. This is true even on the one day of the week that we're not supposed to be so rushed. We hadn't realized how well you're looking; I really don't know when I've seen you looking so fine. Tell us about it. We're almost like one big family anyway, don't you think?"

Thus encouraged, Wun-yung's Mother answered, "You have always been so gentlemanly and kind to me, Wun-sik-ssee. If you're just half as nice to Pawk-soon's Mother, she's a fortunate woman. It's true enough, I have to work longer hours than when Pawk-soon's Mother was helping me. But it's also true that there was no peace in our household then, or prior to that. Now the peace is like that new machinery they have that works so quietly when they drop oil on it. Of course, it's not real oil, but it does soften our noisy voices, and it does drop down on us from the beautiful sky where our Father dwells."

Glossary

Page	Words Referred To	Explanation
8	Kei-myung	One syllable was taken from each high school's name to make the name of the college that later became a university.
12	Wun-yung's Mother	In Korea, for centuries, a mother was not called by her childhood given name, but "mother of (first child's name)." Only recently has this custom partially changed.
15	Saek-ssee	A young woman; occasionally a bride.
16	Wun-sik-ssee	Ssee is an honorific term, used after a given or surname.
17	conversation	Koreans have never eavesdropped at keyholes. At this period in their history, most of the doors in ordinary homes were made of wooden lattice, with one thickness of mulberry pulp paper pasted over it. Shadows and voices were easily seen and heard through the doors.
17	Kim-Teacher	Teacher is simply an honorific term, and is often used that way in Korea, especially when no other title seems to fit.
18	Paek Kee-haw	In several Eastern countries, the surname, or family name, comes first.
19	taw-jahng	The name of the bearer was carved in reverse on a cylindrical, square or oval stone, or at the end of a small, dowel-like piece of hardwood, such as bamboo. Each person carries this with him or her, together with a little covered pad of red ink, for stamping or "signing" any official document.
21	one-kahn	The old unit of measure, used in describing the size of a building; approximately eight-feet square, or sixty-four square feet.
21	mah-jahng	As the lee, (⅓ of a mile) is only used in multiples of five, this term takes care of one through four, six through nine, and so forth.

21	Wun-sik, Wun-sig-ee	A euphonic change from a final k to a hard g occurs before a vowel.
25	chook-cauldron	Chook is a sort of soupy, cereal-like gruel that is cooked for the livestock. Usually it contains barley, milo-maize and/or vegetable remnants. Westerners have used this term, chook, for breakfast cereal.
26	kim-chee	A Korean favorite, fermented brine-pickle, made mainly from Chinese cabbage, highly spiced with red peppers, flavored with garlic and in some areas, a little fish.
26	awn-dawl	Means "hot-stone." The kitchen was built at a lower level than the combination living/dining/bedroom. It was also lower than the yard outside. This makes it possible to construct flues under the flat stones of the floor of the upper room. The kitchen fire(s) thus heats the floor, providing an ancient form of radiant heat to the living quarters.
27	Ah-ee-gaw	Exclamation of surprise or wonder. We might say, "Oh my!"
27	taw-ggae-bee	Goblin, sprite.
28	yung-chig-ee	Phrase repeated by workmen to help synchronize and give rhythm to a group effort.
28	Ah-ee-gaw	Cf. 27
29	rice-flavored-water	The after-meal drink for most people in Korea, water that has been heated in the almost empty rice kettle. This custom, too, may have changed for many city people in recent years.
29	Inside Person	The polite, unpretentious, humble way of speaking of one's wife.
33	haw-mee	Short-handled grubbing hoe.
34	Soon-hee	Her given name is composed of two Chinese characters, one for each syllable. Soon means even-tempered, docile. Hee means happy.
35	Ah-ee-gaw	Cf. 27
36	Korean count	A Korean child is one on the day of birth. When New Year's Day comes, he's two. If he happens to be born the day before New Year's, he's two the next day.

45	clearing his throat	Used instead of ringing or knocking at a door.
46	morning calm	Chosen, (Japanese spelling;) chaw-sun, old name for Korea. Used by the Japanese occupation, so now very unpopular.
48	half-bows	In the Korean half-bow, a man bends his knees a little, with the arms held downwards. The palms of his hands face towards his legs. As he inclines his head forward, his hands also go forward at a level half-way between the normal level of his hands and his feet.
49	full-bows	A full-bow consists in placing the palms of the hands flat on the floor, while dropping first to the left and then to the right knee. Next the man bows forward until his nose almost touches the floor, remaining in that position for two of three seconds. He then raises his head and right knee, and comes on up, hands and left knee leaving the floor simultaneously.
49	jujube	Jujubus Zizyphus, (Chinese date,) a deciduous tree of the Orient, bearing a rather dry fruit, about the size of a date, used in special foods.
51	name implies	Cf. 34.
53	jujube	Cf. 49.
56	lee	Approximately a little over one-third of a mile. Ten lee is about 3 miles. Cf. also 21.
58	Korean count	Cf. 36.
59	rice-water	Cf. 29.
59	Kawng-jah	Korean pronunciation of Confucius, the great Chinese scholar, who lived 551 to 478 B.C.
61	"peace"	Called by Koreans the "Peaceful Ahn" character. The lower part is "yu," meaning woman or female. The upper part looks like a roof, with the ridgepole in the center. In the orient, one woman under a roof, stands for "peace." Hence this book's name.
63	moo-nyu	Sorceress; witch doctor
65	Room of Writing	Or Writing Room. Korean term is Keul-pahng. This term was used for the old-fashioned "School of the Classics."

67	Mee-gook	The Chinese characters, formerly used for the U.S.A., meant Beautiful Country.
74	too-roo-mah-gee	The long, flowing outer-robe that the Korean gentleman wears in public. It is tied in front with two sashes or ribbons in a single bow-knot.
79	Lee Wun-yung	A very remarkable and dedicated minister with this name, actually lived and served in the Kyung-ahn Presbytery, (northern part of N. Kyung-sahng Province,) where, he suffered in prison for his faith for years and died soon after. The author of this novel has borrowed his name, for he was as true a martyr as any, and every Christian should know his name.
81	first-born rascal	A liberal translation of "maht-chah-sik."
81	name like yours	Ahn literally means "peace." This was the Rev. Dr. James Edward Adams' (years of service in Korea, 1895 to 1925), Korean surname; also that of the three sons who served there as missionaries, the Rev. Dr. Edward Adams, (1921 to 1963); the Rev. Benjamin Nyce Adams, (1923 to 1930); and the Rev. George Jacob Adams, (1932 to 1959). Cf. *"History of the Korea Mission Presby. Church in the U.S.A., Volume II."*
85	Outside-Lord	Literal translation of pah-kkaht-choo-een.
86	Eup	County-Seat.
87	mix the ink	The ink-stick would be rubbed on the ink-stone with a few drops of water.
87	Koong-moon	Language of the country, national language.
87	kim-chee	Cf. p. 26
88	mah-dahng	Courtyard
91	Inside Woman	Cf. p. 29.
95	grandmother-flower	A purplish red flower of the buttercup family, genus anemone; without petals, but with colored sepals. The flower stem has a crooked back. After blooming, the white, hairy crown, attached to the seeds, which helps them disseminate, gives it its Korean name.

95	un-duk	A dike; embankment; hill; hillside.
97	taw-jahng	Cf. p. 19.
100	sah-rahng	Or sah-rahng-pahng. The men's parlor. Nicer homes always have one.
101	perfect condition	The author had the self-same experience in the mid-thirties. He was relaxing with a book on the ancient city-wall, which by then had deteriorated to nothing more than a curved hill. It was behind the residence assigned to his family, and several years before that to his brother Ben's family in Ahn-dawng, (Andong.) N. Kyung-sahng Province. He noticed a small, glazed, partly exposed piece of pottery. A little digging unearthed a lovely five-inch vase from the Silla period, 57 B.C. to 935 A.D.
102	yah-dahn	Uproar, racket, row.
109	great scholar	Mencius, Chinese, lived 372 to 289 B.C.
109	mind with suffering	VI 2:15.2 If the reader is fortunate enough to locate a volume of the writings of Mencius, the reference will help him/her to find the quotation.
109	Honorable Confucius	Chinese scholar, lived 551 to 479 B.C.
109	will have neighbors	4:25, "Writings of Confucius."
110	"Yes, I'm going"	Literal translation, Korean vernacular.
111	too-roo-mah-gee	Cf. p. 74.
112	cash (p'oon)	Round coins with square holes in the center, usually strung on small straw rope. Beast of burden needed to carry enough for any large transaction.
115	Ah-ee-gaw	Cf. p. 27.
116	Older brother	Respectful and friendly way of addressing an older man.
118	Lord-man	Literal translation of choo-een, the Master of the house; the head of a family; one's husband.
119	maht-chah-sik	Cf. p. 81.
120	go tomorrow	English: come to our place; . . . come tomorrow.
123	poo-jah	Rich persons, people; millionaires.
123	going	coming, Cf. 110.
125	kahn	Space measuring approximately 8 feet by 8 feet. Also Cf. 21.
126	nah	Korean letter "n"

127	chee-ge	An A-frame, portable back-rack. Two long legs permit it to be lowered to the ground and to be supported upright with a forked stick. Tremendous loads are carried thus by one man.
127	cow	Bulls and cows, (native stock), are used for draft purposes.
128	kee-doong	Upright squared posts; pillars.
128	moon	Much of rural Korea has for centuries operated by the lunar calendar.
129	heavy straw-mats	Heavy straw-mats were usually 7 to 8 feet square.
130	East Mountain	The mission hospital on the west side of Tae-goo, is still called the East Mountain Hospital. Cf. photograph, p. 122.
135	Rev. Lee Wun-yung	Cf. p. 79.
140	mah-jahng	Cf. p. 21.
140	1,000 x 10,000	Expression used for "You're welcome!" "Don't mention it!" Or in other words, "You're exaggerating it ten million times."
141	poo-jah	Cf. p. 123.
141	choo-mu-nee	Money pouch with drawstring. This word was also sometimes used for pocket.
144	ten-chun piece	In those days, in the early years of the 20th century, 100 chun was one wun, (won), which was worth about 50 cents U.S.A.
151	U-mu-nee	Mother.
152	chee-ge	Cf. p. 127.
152	mah-jahng	Cf. p. 21.
152	pah-chee-ge	A woven, basket-like container, which on occasion is fastened inside the chee-ge forks, enabling the bearer to carry small packages or unwrapped articles. Though not the usual way, if well padded, a small baby could be safely carried in it, as the author's children have been.
159	Lady of Peace	He simply punned on the name she was usually called, Ahn Poo-een, (Lady). Cf. pp. 61 and 81.
160	grandmother flowers	Cf. p. 95.
164	let down the mind	Very literal translation. "Put down" might be even better.

168	Outside-Lord	The Korean expression is pahkk-**kaht'** choo-een. Cf. p. 85.
169	Writing Room	Cf. p. 65.
171	Yu-baw	The literal meaning is "Look here", but by usage and connotation it has come to mean "hello," "here," or "friend."
171	too-roo-mahk	Cf. p. 88.
172	chah	Korean foot measure, 3.03 decimeters.
172	lantern's	Probably burned whale oil, or possibly kerosene; and had paper sides to let the light through.
173	to be yours	Divorce was seldom heard of. In the case of a second wife or concubine, if there was dissatisfaction, she was simply returned to her parent's home.
174	chook	Cf. p. 25.
175	un-duk	Cf. p. 95.
175	Great School	University.
176	moo-nyu	Cf. p. 63
176	yahk	Medicine.
184	tawk	Large, Ali Baba-type, earthenware jars used for water and winter kim-chee storage. Cf. 26.
184	persimmons	Exposure to frost reduces or eliminates their astringency.
184	Pawk-soon-ee	Pawk means blessing; and soon means docility.
184	kim-chee-tawk	Cf. tawk, above.
186	kerosene cans	In those days kerosene was sold to merchants in 5-gal. tin cans. After retailing the kerosene, the cans were sold and used in many ways.